HOW TO MARRY

TO MARRY

the

WRONG GUY

How to Marry *the* Wrong Guy

A Guide for Avoiding the Biggest Mistake of Your Life

Anne Milford

Jennifer Gauvain, MSW, LCSW

coldfeetpress.com

Editor: Leslie Gibson McCarthy

Copyeditors: David Brumfield, Tim Gauvain and Rebekah Matt

Consultant: Christine Frank, www.christinefrank.com

Cover and Interior design: Shelley Dieterichs, www.artbyshelley.com

Author photos: Linda Rivard, www.rivardphotography.com

ISBN: 978-0-615-27419-5

First Printing, May 2009

Printed in the United States of America

Contents

How to Marry the Wrong Guy

This book is dedicated to all the women who shared
their stories ... and to all the women who need to hear them.

Preface

It was 5 p.m. on a warm Sunday in July, and my fiance was scolding me for being late. He was upset that I was not going to have time to pack our picnic dinner for the concert that night. He stood there in a bathrobe, unshaved and unshowered, after a full day spent in front of the television. Time slowed while I reflected on my day of travel: two hours in the car to the Orlando airport, rental car return, baggage check, tedious tram ride and the cattle call for the wide-body L-1011 aircraft jam-packed with 250 passengers. Then the whole process in reverse when I arrived in Chicago, including an hour in traffic getting back to his house. (Note to self: Don't most couples in love pick each other up at the airport?) I can still picture him lecturing me about how I "would never have time to go to the store and get what we need for dinner." The whole situation was so crazy that I didn't bother to mention three key things that seemed to escape him: There are no stores at 35,000 feet; there was nothing I could have done to make the plane fly faster; and what the hell had he been doing all day?

I once heard a therapist use the analogy of a beach ball. She said your problems are like a beach ball that you keep trying to hold under water. You can try to ignore them, but eventually those problems, just like a beach ball, are going to pop up out of the water. This was the day that my beach ball finally popped out of the water. Five days later, I called off the engagement and moved back home. It was the Fourth of July — Independence Day.

When I was 28, I became engaged to a man who was completely and utterly wrong for me. For reasons that remain unclear, I fully participated in a relationship that was doomed from the start, contrary to all my gut feelings, and covered with red flags. Fortunately, I found the courage to call off the wedding before I got myself into a bigger mess.

After I called off the wedding, I moved back to my hometown, found a new job, and got an apartment. My sweet friends were worried about me and went out of their way to make sure I was doing Ok. While I felt somewhat embarrassed by my poor judgment, I was so happy to be free that my joy at being back home and out of that bad relationship outweighed any shame or sadness. The hardest part was facing up to the situation and making the tough call to get out.

As I talked to other people about my unfortunate engagement, I started hearing the same comments over and over. First, I was surprised by the number of people who admitted they wished they had the courage to call off their own wedding. I even had several people (of all ages) admit to short-lived first marriages that no one knew about. I also began to see a pattern develop as people started to ask me the same questions about my relationship: *What were the signs? How did I feel? How did I have the courage to call it off? How did my fiance react?* I quickly realized that in many cases, they were really questioning their own relationship or pending marriage. After a while, I had mentally catalogued a collection of personal stories about doomed-from-the-start marriages and faced another gut feeling — this needs to be a book. As a freelance writer, an avid reader, and a person who spends hours in bookstores and libraries, I couldn't help but notice shelves filled with rows and rows of books about how to plan a successful wedding. Countless books promise to help women "hook a man," or "find your soulmate in thirty days." It drove me crazy to see some of these books — women are so much smarter than this! They deserve better. What they really need is a book that helps them step back and evaluate what they want and need in their relationships.

I could have used such a book; it would have saved me a lot of heartache. That's when I had my epiphany. Who better to tell you how to extricate yourself from a dead-end relationship than a woman who has done time in one? *No one* is better informed about unhealthy relationships than a woman who has learned the hard way. That was it! I realized that my experience of calling off a wedding could really help other women. And I could uncover what a woman needs to know about marrying the *right* guy by talking to women who had married the *wrong* one! So I set out to find answers to the following:

- **Why do women stay in relationships that they know are all wrong for them?**
- **Why do smart, talented, successful, worthy women *consciously* get engaged to the wrong guy?**
- **Why do they walk down that aisle even though they *already* know it is a mistake?**

The first step was finding women to interview. Each woman I talked to had to meet one standard prior to being interviewed: Did she know she was making a mistake BEFORE she walked down the aisle? That way I knew I would be interviewing women who:

1. Settled for a ho-hum (or even destructive), less-than-fulfilling relationship, and then . . .

2. Went through with her wedding even though she knew it was a mistake.

It didn't take long to find the first 30 women who fit the profile. I sent out a mass e-mail to my friends, relatives, neighbors, and colleagues explaining this project along with a questionnaire. I got a big response and started receiving completed questionnaires or e-mails indicating that a person was willing to be interviewed. I got even more responses from those I sent the e-mails to saying they knew someone who fit the criteria, but were afraid to contact her for fear of prying or being insensitive.

The amazing thing is that I didn't have to travel more than a few "degrees of separation" to find qualified candidates to interview. This told me I was on to something. In all cases, these women agreed to revisit these very personal and often painful memories to help someone else. Every single woman said something to the effect of, "If I can help prevent someone else from making the same mistake, it is worth reliving these painful memories."

At this point in the research, I had the great fortune to begin my collaboration with Jennifer K. Gauvain, MSW, LCSW. Jennifer is a licensed therapist whose primary focus is helping couples and families. With over 15 years' experience in private practice, she helped me interpret the stories I gathered and address the issues revealed by those who forged ahead with a mistaken marriage. She also shared the wisdom she and gained from enduring her own parents' painful divorce.

After conducting the interviews and poring over the data, something remarkable occurred. No matter what the women's background, age, education level, or religious affiliation, they all gave startlingly similar reasons for why they remained in their unfulfilling relationship or went ahead with a mistaken marriage. While they were very different in many ways, they all echoed the same advice: "Listen to your gut," or "Pay attention to that little voice inside of you." They talked about their gut feelings over and over, so we decided to look further into this concept of gut feelings.

Jennifer and I also decided to track down women who *did* listen to their gut — women who had canceled a wedding and ended a dead-end relationship. When we set out to find them, something interesting occurred as well. We quickly realized that it was *much harder* to find women who had called off a wedding. And many people that we did find ultimately declined to speak about this time in their life. They did not want to "go there" again and dredge up all of those painful memories. It took us a while, but we eventually conducted interviews and again found common themes and patterns in their stories. The difference was that they were somehow able to dial in to their inner wisdom and find the courage to act on these feelings. They called it off.

By presenting real-life stories, coupled with research and professional insight, we hope that a potential bride who is headed down the aisle to disaster will recognize herself in one of these stories and stop short before she makes a life-altering mistake. We also want to reach the woman who is enmeshed in an unhappy relationship simply because she doesn't want to be alone. As one woman said about her 26-year-old assistant, "I wish I could bottle up all the feelings I had during my mistaken marriage and give them to her so she could see where she is headed in her own unhealthy relationship. I have talked to her until I am blue in the face about how wrong her fiancé is for her but she doesn't want to 'waste the six years' invested in the relationship!"

The good news is that every woman in this book went on to a happy and fulfilling Act II — after she ended her marriage or engagement. It wasn't the lonely and dismal future she envisioned when she was in the middle of the storm. By sharing these real stories, we hope to spare others the anguish, guilt, and sadness of a failed marriage.

We also hope that someone who is in a potentially unhealthy or unfulfilling relationship identifies what it is she is really looking for and establishes a way to find it. As Robert Frost eloquently said, "The best way out is always through." The stories you are about to read are true. Our hope is that by reading them, a part of you will recognize yourself and be triggered to act. That part of you that has been *longing* to be heard. This is your opportunity to finally listen to what you *already* know is true. Through these stories, you will find your way out.

Anne Milford
Jennifer Gauvain
March, 2009

No, I don't!

Picture yourself in a little chapel, or synagogue, or glorious cathedral. You are a bride. You are minutes away from saying "I do," but you really want to scream, "No, no, I don't!" Your heart is racing and you've got butterflies in your stomach — and they're not the good kind. <u>You are freaking out</u>. You know you are about to marry the wrong man. What's going through your mind?

I was standing at the end of the aisle thinking "Shit, when am I going to get divorced?"

I kept listening for the music — and the ushers never opened the door. I finally pushed it open myself, like it was a grand performance. I walked down the aisle looking at all of my friends and family whom I did not want to disappoint. At the reception I thought — "Oh my God, what have I done?" I realized I had no emotional attachment to this man.

I was avoiding my dad's eyes as I waited with him at the end of the aisle — I did not want to hear any "pearls of wisdom." Instead I paid attention to the photographer — I simply could not look at my dad because I knew I was making a mistake.

I was scared to death. I wanted to turn around and run — it felt so surreal, like it was something I was watching and not a part of.

I barely remember the wedding ceremony; it was very simple and it was not special. We didn't even have a honeymoon. I did what I thought I deserved at the time. I was totally settling.

I don't remember participating in the wedding at all. I never did, even in the months and years immediately afterward. I remember speaking to my new husband's grandmother and aunt at the reception when they complimented me on my dress. I spoke to them as if I were in a daze. That's the only thing I remember until we arrived in that town where we were to spend our first night together, about 40 miles from the church.

I was positively numb and felt like I was in the school play — it was surreal.

As I walked down the aisle, I was thinking, WHY AM I HERE? I felt I was too young to get married. (I wasn't — I was 26!) I was also telling myself that I was never going to have sex with another man again, our sex life was terrible, and our relationship was terrible . . . why am I here?

I felt like I was dying a thousand deaths. I just wanted to get the whole thing over with.

The best-kept secret at the wedding

And so we begin with what's often the best-kept secret at the wedding. What is it? It's that the bride <u>knew her marriage was a mistake as she was walking down the aisle.</u> That's right, at the church or the synagogue or the wedding chapel — she already knew her marriage was not going to work. In most cases, we are not talking about spur-of-the-moment, Las Vegas weddings. We are talking about marriages that occur after a period of dating (often lengthy) and engagement.

The quotes you are reading are the actual thoughts of brides who knew they were marrying the wrong guy. We asked them to share what was going through their minds in the moments before the wedding ceremony began. Not the loving, dream-come-true visions of a happy wedding day, are they? Imagine having to put on a happy face and feign unbridled joy—with all eyes on you. What's worse is that the majority of the guests are friends and relatives who have known you for years, if not your whole life. You really have to put on the performance of a lifetime to fool these people. And of course, everyone else has expectations of how the bride should appear on the "happiest day of her life."

In all of the pictures, I was walking ahead of him — not side by side. I spent all my time talking to my cousins and hanging out with my gay friend, the pianist.

For those who believed (actually *convinced themselves*) that marriage was what they really wanted, the reality of the day did not match their "dreams" — misguided as they were. Their wedding day did not turn out the way they had always imagined it to be.

I hated the best man at our wedding. At our rehearsal dinner, I overheard my future mother-in-law in the corner talking to the best man, trying to get him to stop the wedding. She said, "You must stop this! He is making the biggest mistake of his life!" When I told my soon-to-be husband, he said, "Just ignore her."

My wedding day was one of the worst days of my life — my groom got bombed, completely shit-faced. At one point he kicked a chair out from under someone and screamed "FUCK YOU!" at one of the guests. Of course I had to take care of it.

And the worst part of all? — It was too late to turn back. While their insides told them to run away, their outside kept marching down the aisle. Unfortunately, too many people get so caught up with the idea of being "in love" or "being married" that they forget about the most important part — the relationship itself.

The worst-kept secret at the wedding

And sometimes it's *not* just the bride who knows the marriage is a mistake. Her friends, family, and wedding party know it's all wrong, too. It's like watching a car go over a cliff. Think about it: have you ever been to a wedding and placed a silent bet that the marriage wouldn't last? And it doesn't have to be anything dramatic. Both the bride and groom can be wonderful people — they're just not wonderful for each other.

There was a lot of crying at my wedding. Myself, my friends, my dad. None of us said that it was because of a looming mistake, but it was crying for loss, not for joy.

The women you will meet in this book shared a secret: *I know I am marrying the wrong guy.* But instead of facing their fears in the early stages of their relationship (the fear of being alone, of letting their families down, of being labeled a "failure," of not knowing what the future would bring), they all walked down the aisle anyway. They're sharing their stories with you here in the hope that you will avoid the tough lessons that they had to learn. We're also sharing the wisdom of those who *did* find the courage to call off their wedding. And finally, we spoke to happily married women. Women who have been married for many years and understand the importance of marrying the *right* man. They share their insights about what's important to consider when choosing your husband. They caution that some guys may make a great boyfriend, but a not-so-great husband.

Going with your gut

We believe that deep down, every woman knows what is right for her. Whenever we make a decision or evaluate a situation — big or small — our gut usually lets us know whether we are right or wrong. No matter what you call gut feelings — intuition, sixth sense, inner wisdom — we all have them and it is important to pay attention to what they are telling us.

The women we interviewed kept stressing the importance of "listening to your gut." They all said that they ignored their gut feelings, and that it was one of their biggest mistakes. The hard part is paying attention and taking action! Our goal is that this book will help *any* woman who is having doubts about her relationship or pending marriage to listen to her gut, recognize red flags, and find the courage to do what is right for her.

Here are some important things to keep in mind as you read this book

1. We are not kidding when we say that there are four steps required to marry the wrong man. Every single woman who married the wrong guy completed all four steps — without exception. (See Chapters 1-4.)

2. The women we interviewed were of many different ages, races, and religious backgrounds as well as diverse educational and socioeconomic circumstances. They also come from different parts of the United States. Their stories, however, are remarkably similar. This tells us that these thought patterns, behaviors, and mistakes are universal. Please pay attention to them.

3. We believe that every woman knows, deep down, what is right for her. We hope these stories will serve as a wake-up call to help you recognize your own hazardous relationship patterns and behaviors.

4. If you think that this book does not apply to you because you are not in a relationship or not yet engaged — please think again. The collective wisdom found in these pages can help you better articulate your vision for what you want out of your life. What kind of relationship do you want? What are the important characteristics that you desire in a boyfriend or husband? Do you want to get married? It's important to establish whether or not you want to get married in the first place. Maybe you don't — and it's something else you are really looking for.

5. We hope that these stories will trigger you to take action. Every bad boyfriend that gets dumped, every wacky wedding that gets canceled, every disputed diamond that is returned to the jeweler will be considered a success story!

6. Don't be afraid to mark up this book. Turn back the corners of the pages, underline, highlight, and ask yourself the questions you find in each chapter. This will help you uncover the truth. Let's start with the first set of questions. Please keep them in mind as you move through the book:

- Are you settling for a relationship that does not fulfill you?
- Do you recognize yourself in any of these stories?
- Are you ignoring red flags in your current relationship?
- What is your gut telling you about your current relationship?
- Are your cold feet trying to tell you something?
- Do you want to end your relationship but are afraid to be alone?
- Are you trying to talk yourself *out* of canceling your wedding (even though you know you should)?
- Do you want to get married? If so, why?
- What kind of vision do you have for your married life?

**Ultimately, the answers and the solutions lie within you.
This book will help you find them.**

Why are all the quotes anonymous?

You may have noticed – or will soon – that there are no names attached to the quotes in this book. This was a difficult decision for us to make. The women we spoke with are quite real, and their stories are here in their own words ... so why not provide even first names?

First and most importantly, almost all of the women requested anonymity. They agreed to be interviewed, to fill out questionnaires, to answer highly personal questions and give honest answers, but they clearly wanted their individual identities to remain private. This subject, for most of them, was not pleasant to remember and talk about, no matter how many years ago it happened.

So why *did* they talk? For one reason and one reason only: *to help women like you*. To help you see the warning signs, to give you the courage to back out of a relationship or an engagement that would result in a disastrous marriage. To prevent you from the heartache they went through.

We did consider attaching pseudonyms to each quote, but it turned out to be cumbersome and (we felt) distracting. The women are real. Their stories are real. We respect their privacy and thank them for letting you hear their stories. We think that after reading this book, you will wish that you could thank them, too.

How do you
MARRY
the
WRONG GUY?

Chapter 1

Step 1: Date the wrong person for the wrong reasons

If you marry the wrong person for the wrong reasons, then no matter how hard you work, it's never going to work, because then you have to completely change yourself, completely change them, completely — by that time, you're both dead.
Anne Bancroft

Why would you marry the wrong guy?

Do women *know* they are marrying the wrong guy? Do they know it's a mistake when they are walking down the aisle? The answer to both of those questions is a resounding YES! Why do they do it? Based on all of our interviews, the same unhealthy chain of events drives otherwise intelligent women down the aisle with the wrong guy. They all say yes when they really want to shout NO!

How does this happen? In many cases, it starts when they settle for a less-than-fulfilling relationship. They know it's not right — yet they stay. They plod along, ignoring their gut feelings and the obvious red flags. They fall into a rut. They invest time with someone who is not right for them. In other cases, it's just a matter of timing. They say, "It's time for me to get married." They decide to turn their next date or boyfriend into "the one." But he's not "the one," and deep down they know it. Even so, they ignore that inner voice and the next thing they know, they're standing at the end of the aisle wondering, "How did I get here?"

They know it's wrong and they marry him anyway

We all make mistakes. We forget to add the baking soda to our cookie dough. We run a red light. We open our mouth and ruin the surprise party. We get distracted or don't pay attention. These are little slip-ups with minor repercussions, and we recognize our mistakes *after* the fact. When it comes to dating, though, we've discovered that women often *know* he's the wrong guy. But they *choose* to stay in an unfulfilling relationship. So we decided to explore the following:
1. Why do women stay in a relationship that is not right for them?
2. Why do women push these relationships towards marriage?
3. Why do women go through with the wedding when they know it's a mistake?

Are you dating the wrong person?

There are many reasons why we shut out that little voice that is trying to warn us that something is amiss. What are they? We asked dozens of women: *Why did you remain in an unhealthy relationship or settle for someone with whom you were not genuinely compatible?*

When we evaluated their responses, common themes and patterns emerged. These patterns were predominantly related to feelings of insecurity, loneliness, or external pressure. Here is what they told us, organized by theme:

Insecurity

I wanted the approval of an older man.

I had feelings of unworthiness — my relationship made me feel better about myself.

He exuded characteristics I did not have — he was confident and cool.

I stayed with the relationship because of my own insecurities and because of emotional abuse. He also made me feel like I couldn't make it on my own. My ex-husband was a link to my deceased sister and I thought that if I ended it with him the link would be gone, so I tolerated him berating me and I believed him that I was a bad person. I lost my sister in a traumatic car accident and my parents never initiated therapy. (I was in the car five minutes before it wrecked and was first on the scene.) My ex would give me just enough emotion for me to want more; therefore, the emotional abuse cycle was not broken.

He made me feel really loved — he was very charismatic.

I stayed with him due to the same old insecurities; I think I have a strong need to be loved and to love.

I was needy and lacked self-confidence despite my professional success. I sought to fill that gap with a man.

I thought I was lucky to be with him. I could learn a lot from him.

In my family, I saw that success meant attracting a lot of men. I sort of did that — I got a man because I couldn't support myself without one.

Loneliness
I think it was partial desperation—I wanted to love someone and I wanted someone to love me.

I did not want to keep "floundering" in my life all by myself

External pressures
My age (28) was creeping up on me and I was not dating much — so I was attracted to him.

I was not that happy with my day-to-day life. Six of my good friends from college were married already and I wanted to be married, too. When I met him, I immediately set my sights on him and decided he was good marriage material. That was it.

I wasn't very happy in my professional life. I didn't like my job and was unclear about what to do next. I was sort of in a rut. I think that is why I was susceptible to a poorly-thought-out relationship.

All of my friends were dating seriously or getting married and I thought that I should be in a serious relationship, too. I think I subconsciously planned on getting serious with the next person that came along. It didn't really matter who it was.

Other reasons
I felt maternal instincts for him. "I can fix you — I can be your hero, your savior."

I was physically attracted to him. I was attracted to him because he was attracted to me.

I felt safe and comfortable with the familiar.

I had delusions it would all work out.

I convinced myself I could make any relationship work — I would be whoever I needed to be to make it work.

Taking an empty relationship to the next level

The next event that leads to marital misfortune occurs when the woman (sometimes it's the boyfriend) starts pushing for marriage. Or they view marriage as the next logical step in their relationship. This begs the question: *Why do women push an empty or ineffective relationship towards engagement and marriage?* Or — why do they allow themselves to be passively "pulled along" and become engaged and get married? In some cases, the women we interviewed had pressured their boyfriends to become engaged. In other cases, they felt pulled along — like it "just happened" to them. Again, those same patterns of insecurity, loneliness and external pressure emerged. However, two more themes appeared. One was related to financial insecurity and the other was the amount of time already invested in the relationship.

Again, here is what they told us, organized by theme:

Insecurity
I think I needed to prove something to the rest of my family. If I got married, it would prove that I was better than them. (Everyone in my family was divorced.)

I thought this would be my one chance to get married; I didn't want to risk letting it go.

Loneliness
I was scared to be alone.

I was really still in love with my former boyfriend; he was my best friend and we had lived together. We had a wonderful relationship, but deep down I knew he was gay. We were just like Will and Grace! When I ended that relationship, I immediately fell into another one, even though I was still in love with my old boyfriend. I guess I just didn't want to be alone — that's why I married the wrong man.

I was lonely, scared, and living on loans and grants and fellowships. I was pursuing my graduate degree and had no money, no contacts, and no car. I was from a small town and this was the first time I had been away from home.

External pressures
Half my friends were married and I wanted to be married, too.

People were asking me — why aren't you married? I was tired of that question and felt embarrassed by it.

I wanted to be married and he seemed like a nice guy and my family adored him.

All of my friends were getting married or had very serious relationships. It seemed like everyone I knew from high school, college, and work was married or getting married. I guess I felt left out and thought that I better find someone, too.

Financial
I thought marriage would solve my problems; specifically I would not have to work anymore. I could quit my job.

I saw my fiance as security — he made good money. I relied on that because I was so miserable at my job.

There was the complicating factor of thinking that this was my only acceptable option in life. I didn't have enough money for college because only wealthy people went to college. This in spite of the fact that I was in the top 10 percent of my graduating class — no one told me about scholarships or the fact that people can work their way through college. I was so oblivious to the options, I didn't even know enough to ask questions. No one else in my family had ever been to college except my older brother who started junior college, but never finished. I hated my father and I couldn't wait to move out of his house, but had no money to do so, of course. I saw, as my only other option to marriage, continuing to live with my family and work at the local bank. If I got married, I would live in the country and milk cows. Believe it or not, I really enjoyed that. I also thought that while his family seemed a little weird, I would eventually learn to please them and thereby earn their love. That was appealing to me. I don't know why I thought I had to get married to do that — I didn't think about just getting a job as a cow herder.

Time invested in relationship
I felt like he didn't want to get married all that much, but we had dated for seven years, and lived together for two years, so I said, "Shouldn't we get married at this point in our extensive courtship?" He agreed, and we got engaged.

We were together for eight years. All my friends were getting married and I didn't want to be an old maid.

We had been together for so long. I didn't want to throw all those years of my life away.

I felt I "owed him"— he stayed with me during my cancer treatments.

Other
I was 26 and that was the age I always thought I'd get married and think about starting a family. (Fortunately, we never had kids!)

I was an optimist. I convinced myself that love can conquer anything.

Why do people proceed with the marriage?

Why does a woman go through with a marriage that she already knows is a mistake? Why does she say "I do" when she really wants to shout "I don't"? We asked the following question: Why did you go through with your wedding even though you knew it was a mistake? This time the common themes were a little more complex. They included the fear of letting friends or family down, being too caught up in the momentum of the event (or feeling that it was too late to call it off), the romance of "being a bride," denial, fear of not finding someone else to marry (that this was their one and only chance to marry), and the belief that the relationship would improve after the wedding. Let's take a closer look:

Fear of letting others down
They were all involved in the wedding planning (family and friends) because I had made promises and now I had to carry through. I felt that I couldn't let everyone down. It was that simple in my youthful mind.

I felt so guilty — I did not want to let my family down. What is interesting is that my parents would have totally supported me. All of my energy was directed at finishing school at this point, so I just went ahead with it because I couldn't deal with this particular problem at the time.

I had observed my sister making many mistakes and getting in a lot of trouble. I didn't want to do anything wrong — I never did anything wrong. I felt I couldn't call it off; that would be the "wrong thing" to do. The ironic part is my mom would have completely supported me if I had. In fact, she gave me ample opportunity to cancel the wedding.

Several times I wanted to call off the wedding but didn't want to disappoint my friends at college or my family, so I thought it would work. I liked my fiance, but love? Not really.

Caught up in momentum of the wedding/it was too late to call it off
I did want to call off the wedding, but I just felt swept along. I wanted to keep everyone happy.

I did not want to let everyone down by canceling the wedding — my friends, my family, and my fiance.

Romance of "being a bride"
I was excited about the idea of being a bride and getting married — and he said he loved me.

Everyone else was getting married. I was in a sorority and there was a ceremony that took place every time someone got engaged. Everyone was checking out bridesmaid dresses. There was a lot of pressure.

Denial
I was in total denial! My friends were all married with babies and I wanted to do the same. I discounted the fact that he was all wrong for me, I completely ignored it.

I knew it was not going to work before the wedding — he never wanted to have sex. I convinced myself I did not need a sexual relationship.

Fear of not finding someone else to marry/this was the one and only chance
I wondered if anyone else would want to marry me. I also wondered if there would ever be another person that I would want to marry.

I thought he was so good looking. I never thought that I would get the chance to marry someone like him.

I almost called it off. I started hanging out with another guy and really liked him, but I was scared to death. I started feeling like I was never going to get married. I was very conflicted. At the same time I was exploring the new relationship, my fiance ended up in the hospital and I went to his bedside to visit him. I was pulled back into the relationship and that was it. I ended it with the other guy and went through with the wedding.

Belief that the relationship would improve after the wedding
Even though the "bloom was off the rose" already, I thought that things would get better once we were married.

I didn't think that he would change; I just hoped that I could change enough to make him happy someday — that someday he would find me worthy of a compliment (or at least stop finding fault with me).

I desperately wanted to be married. I told myself he would be different after marriage.
I have never figured out why I continued to stay with him. We were friends and enjoyed one another's company at times. Our sex was not enough for me; our relationship was not enough for me. I think it was the first time I decided to be in a committed relationship. I thought that we had to grow and change; that things would change after we were married. I still don't know.

I really wanted a family and I didn't realize at the time that you can't change someone. I really thought he would change.

Unwilling to admit mistake/embarrassment
I did not want to admit I had made a huge mistake and kept thinking I could make things work. I did not want the embarrassment of calling off a planned wedding.

Two things stopped me from calling it off. The first was pride; I did not want to admit that my parents were right (they had never liked my fiance) and I did not want to admit that I had made a mistake.

Other reasons
I was so young . . . I thought that what others thought mattered a lot. I was also pregnant and fearful of what he would do if I did not marry him. He threatened to take my baby from me.

He was not a great guy, but for some reason I had it bad for him. He was attracted to me and it was easy to be enraptured by him. He also was the first man I had sex with and this played a part in it, for sure.

He pursued me and was a man of the world (or so I thought at the time). He had a lot of money and he bought me clothes, dressed me, and told me how to wear my hair and what color to dye my hair. (In hindsight I know this is a hallmark of abuse/dysfunction.) I was just so attracted to this loyalty he showed me — his pursuit and the perceived devotion.

Sleepwalking into marriage

Many women we spoke with described themselves as being "passively pulled along" towards marriage. A few remember feeling as if they were "sleepwalking" or in a "surreal" state of being. Charlotte Mayerson, the author of *Goin' to the Chapel: Dreams of Love, Realities of Marriage*, uses this exact term, "sleepwalking", to describe how many women walk into a marriage without considering what kind of husband they need in order to have the kind of marriage they want. Mayerson interviewed women from across the United States, of all ages and walks of life about how they viewed their married lives. Based on her extensive conversations, she identified two distinctly different attitudes that impacted the success and happiness of a marriage. She labeled these women as either "dreamers" or "calculators." According to Mayerson, the dreamers had not consciously outlined the characteristics that were important to them. She says these women usually had some vision for their married life, but they did not quantify what type of man they needed to fulfill this vision. For example, a young woman with a strong religious faith dreams of raising a large family in the suburbs. She pictures a life filled with church suppers, school activities and plenty of family time. Her current boyfriend is an avowed agnostic who doesn't think he wants children. He loves his career as a stock trader and expects his wife to have a high-powered career, too. Do you think her dreams will be realized with this man? What about the woman who loves her fast-paced lifestyle? She pictures herself in a high-rise condominium, in downtown Chicago. She can see her husband by her side as they explore everything the city has to offer — theatres, museums, and great restaurants. Don't you think she better think twice before marrying her current fiance: a self-described homebody, whose favorite pastime is watching televised sports? These men are not going to change; neither are the women. Why should they? In the short term, these marriages might work; but in the long run the odds are stacked against them.

The man you want to spend *your* life with is the man who shares a similar vision for the future. Paying attention to what you want out of your life together *after* you get married leads to . . . umm, well. . . DIVORCE. Listen to these words of wisdom from a 66 year old, self described "dreamer" who was a part of Mayerson's study:

> "When it was time to get married, along came this guy who was handsome and a great athlete — just like my dopey dreams. So I married him. I never thought about it in terms of what life was all about. I didn't say, 'Is he going to make a good husband? Are we going to have a good life together? Do we have the same ideals? Will he be able to earn a living? Be proud of himself?' None of that. Absolutely none." [i]

After so many tales of divorce from the dreamers, Mayerson's undeniable conclusion is that the majority of women who failed to consider the qualities they desired in a husband had unhappy first marriages. On the flip side, the women who *did* qualify what they wanted in a husband — the calculators — were much more likely to have a happy marriage. Her interviews revealed that these women understood that their choice of husband played a key role in whether or not they would have a happy and fulfilling life.

Are you a dreamer or a calculator?

- Have you dreamed about your wedding and marriage since you were a little girl?
- Have you given any thought to the characteristics you want in a husband?
- If so, does your boyfriend or fiance have these characteristics?

Being described as a "calculating woman" can be perceived as negative. But what it actually means is that you have practically and thoughtfully considered all of the important characteristics you desire in your future spouse, or in a long-term relationship. It also means that you have thought about your vision for your married life. If it takes being labeled a calculator to build a happy and satisfying marriage or relationship, wear that label with pride.

It will lead you to take a long, hard look at whether or not your current boyfriend or fiance meets those qualifications. It will also give you the facts you need to recognize whether or not a relationship will work (and the courage to end it if it won't.)

Remaining in a relationship that is not right for both of you

A relationship does not have to include dishonesty, infidelity, or disrespect to be wrong. Two perfectly wonderful people can be in a relationship and simply be wrong *for each other*. We heard it again and again. "That little voice kept telling me this was all wrong, but I struggled with ending it because he was a good person." Or, "He had so many good qualities, but I just didn't feel that spark." This seems to be a major source of confusion and anxiety. Women talk themselves out of what they know is right. They are conflicted about breaking up with a nice boyfriend, even though the electricity or chemistry is missing. They tell themselves that they should stay because their partner is not a cheater or a liar. There's no drama (which is a good thing) but deep down they know that the relationship is not all that it should be.

Unfortunately, remaining in a relationship that is not right is a major disservice to *both* partners. You don't bring out the best in each other. You remain stagnant. You don't grow in your partnership. You miss opportunities for personal transformation, such as a new career, a move to a new city, or trying a new hobby, all because you are tied to someone who is not right for you. The worst part is that it will keep you from meeting someone really great.

It seems so obvious, doesn't it? If your relationship is unhappy, boring, unhealthy, and stressful during courtship, it makes sense to assume that it will be exactly the same way after you get married. Probably worse. (Strike that — it *definitely* will be worse.) So why continue? Even if you are not yet talking marriage, why are you dating someone who you *already* know is not right for you? Why are you wasting your time?

Let's turn those questions around that we asked at the beginning of this chapter:

1. Are you in a relationship that is not right for you?
2. Are you pushing (or being pulled along in) a relationship that is hurtling towards engagement and marriage?
3. Are you going forward with a wedding (and marriage) that you know is a mistake?

i Charlotte Mayerson, *Goin' to the Chapel: Dreams of Love, Realities of Marriage* (New York Basic Books, 1996), 32.

Chapter 2

Step 2: Convince yourself that marriage will solve all your problems

And You Wonder "Why It Didn't Last"

She married him because he was such a "strong man."
She divorced him because he was such a "dominating male."
He married her because she was so "fragile and cute."
He divorced her because she was so "weak and helpless."
She married him because "he is a good provider."
She divorced him because "all he thinks about is business."
He married her because "she reminds me of my mother."
He divorced her because "she's getting more like her mother every day."
She married him because he was "happy and romantic."
She divorced him because he was "shiftless and fun-loving."
He married her because she was "steady and sensible."
He divorced her because she was "boring and dull."
She married him because he was "the life of the party."
She divorced him because "he's a party boy."

Author Unknown

Do you think marriage is a solution to your problems?

In the last chapter, we looked at why women date the wrong guy for all the wrong reasons. We also learned why they stayed in these relationships, even though they knew it was not right for them. Now let's take a closer look at why women get married — and why it is often for all the wrong reasons. Many women told us that they believed that marriage would solve their problems —either problems in their relationship or other problems in their life. They told us over and over that they believed marriage would change their relationship and make it better. They also believed that getting married would make them happier, or more fulfilled. What was really eye-opening is that most women seemed to focus more on the *idea* of marriage or the institution of marriage rather than *who* they were marrying.

Here is a scary statistic for you. In the book *The Most Important Year In A Man's Life, The Most Important Year In a Woman's Life*, the authors report that a typical bride will spend between 150-500 hours preparing for her wedding — the equivalent of one to three months working at a full-time job.[i] However, that same bride will only spend about 15 hours preparing for the actual marriage — the relationship with her husband.

These numbers should be reversed. More time should be spent evaluating the relationship. Hundreds of hours should be directed towards determining whether or not the relationship has all the ingredients to withstand the test of time. An engaged couple should spend 150 to 500 hours figuring out how to weather the sickness, not the health, the bad times, not the good, and the poorer, not the richer days of their future marriage. They should also make sure they really want to get married in the first place.

It's important for both partners to have the same goals, beliefs and ideals driving their decision to wed. If they don't, it's a recipe for unhappiness. Everyone we interviewed had the benefit of hindsight and they said the same thing: They realized they got married for all of the wrong reasons.

While I was happy in my professional life, my personal life was not great. I was grasping for change so I began to focus on my personal life. I thought that if I got married I would be happy, even though I wasn't even dating anyone at the time! I thought that marriage was the solution to my unhappiness.

I didn't feel together in my life, I didn't like my job and had no clear career path. I focused on the personal side of my life. Lots of my friends were getting married and dating very seriously. I thought that I should be doing it, too.

We got engaged at the Four Seasons Hotel . . . I was excited, but in hindsight, I just wanted to be engaged to <u>anyone</u>!

Myth: Marriage = Instant Success and Happiness

Does the *act of marrying* really make you happy? Does it set you on the path to happiness? Is it a mark of success and achievement? In her book, *The Starter Marriage and the Future of Matrimony*, author Pamela Paul talks about the statement being married makes to others:

> Getting married sends a strong signal: You've got it all together. You're in control, on top of things. Being married creates a powerful message about who you

are and where you're going, because we assume that once you're wed, the rest falls into place the beautiful home, the gourmet dinner parties attended by other witty, vivacious couples, the glorious pregnancy — with a trouble-free healthy baby its proud result, the child-rearing years complete with nanny and perhaps some part-time work for Mom, comfortably carried out from her home office. The kids who always do their homework and get into prestigious schools, the fabulous family vacations to Tahoe and Paris and the Grand Canyon, and ultimately, home fires burning into the golden years, furnished with grinning grandchildren and oversized family portraits. All you need to do is marry; the attendant rewards are waiting.ⁱⁱ

That sounds a little ridiculous, doesn't it? We know that Paul has her tongue planted firmly in her cheek. But there is some truth in the jest. Marriage often *is* idealized by our society. It also confirms your desirability: "Look! Someone wanted to marry me, so I must be worthwhile." It's easy to fall prey to this myth.

Under pressure—I have to get married now (but I really don't know why)

Another reason people want to marry is due to the unrelenting pressure from their friends, families, and themselves. They also feel financial pressure or the pressure of passing time. Most of the women we interviewed talked about pressure of one form or another that influenced their decision to marry. It didn't matter whether it was self-imposed or external. Either way, it led them to make bad choices. Here is what they told us:

Family pressure
I felt that I had to go through with my wedding. I'm from a large family and I was the only surviving daughter. (My sister had passed away from a car accident). My parents wanted a huge party and a huge party is what they had. My mom and his mom planned the whole thing. All of my friends were getting married and I wanted to have a wedding with him so bad. I pressured him a lot.

Financial pressure

I was raised in an abusive environment. I was used to being abused and hiding it. I failed myself and did not know how to get out. For some reason I felt that living with this person meant I was supposed to stay. I was not in an economic position to support myself (this was a big reason). This was also the first relationship I was really in. I dated in college, but was never in a relationship. I was never interested in settling down, and then suddenly I think I had no direction in life and being in this relationship gave me something.

I was positively floundering, and I wanted to be settled. I was looking around at other women my age and felt that they were floundering too, and I did not want to be like them. So I looked at the man I was dating and thought, this is great! He is older — he is established. (I didn't look close enough because he was 38 years old and living with his mother!) I didn't want to work and thought that I could stay home and have little brown–eyed, brown-haired babies and make play dates like my sister did!

Pressure of passing time

I was getting older and wanted to be married. He seemed like a nice guy and my family just adored him. I know they wanted me to marry him. I suppose I just didn't think it would turn out years later like it did.

Why did I get married to him? We were on the path to marriage and it was simply the next logical step. It all funneled down to this.

I convinced myself that if I don't do this now, with him, I will never get married. I just wanted to have kids and to be a mom.

Career/Lifestyle Pressure

At one point during our engagement my fiance turned to me and said "Do you realize if it weren't for the horses, we would not have anything in common?" That should have been a good indicator, but I was not the type to give up on something and I did truly love him. My line of business is full of travel and is also seasonal, so starting a relationship with someone from the regular working world was hard, if not impossible. Having a relationship with someone in the same business was very attractive and easier to manage. Of course in our close circle of friends and clients we had a lot in common: polo, horses, and a lot of travel.

Everyone I worked with was married or getting married. If you weren't in a serious relationship, you didn't fit in. They were all doing "couple-type" activities such as going to the wineries, dinner parties and weekend getaways. If you weren't part of a couple, you weren't invited.

Pressure to grow up
I wanted to be an adult. I thought by marrying I would become an adult. I didn't know I was already an adult.

Sexual pressure
I felt really guilty because I had sex with him. I was such a good girl and I had already gone to bed with him. That really weighed heavily on me. I thought it would assuage my guilt if I married him.

The problem with pressure

It's hard to think clearly when we are under pressure. No matter what the situation, we tend to make mistakes when we feel rushed, overwhelmed and pressured. It's easy to become confused. When you are feeling anxious about your love life, or trying to meet a self-imposed marital deadline, chances are good that you will marry the wrong guy. That's something to think about. The pressure to marry causes you to pick the wrong guy. Sound familiar? Don't forget, we are talking *the rest of your life* here. It's vitally important to take a step back and carefully observe what's *really* going on. If you're aware of this pressure and can understand what's pressuring you, you can spare yourself a lot of pain. Proceed with caution.

Reality check: Why do you want to get married?

OK, so now it's clear that we are constantly bombarded with confusing messages about marriage and what it will bring us. So what are we really looking for? What do we really need? We are ultimately looking for someone to love us. But what do we mean by love? We have to think very carefully about what our definition of love is. It can't be simply those giddy feelings; butterflies and all that (although that is important —more on that subject later). What we really need is someone who understands us and cares about our well-being. We want to be appreciated and valued. We want to feel adored and respected.

Don't be distracted by the butterflies!

You have to be very careful and look at the big picture. Make sure that your boyfriend doesn't just *tell* you that he loves you. He needs to *show* you that he loves you, too. Don't be distracted by the butterflies. Someone who really loves and cherishes you does not drink too much or have affairs. One woman told us:

My ex really made me feel loved — he was and still is very charismatic. I totally believed in him and gave him everything I had even though he was drinking too much and having affairs. He was very intense — the best and the worst. It was almost impossible for me to walk away. And like many women, I wondered if anyone else would ever want to marry me or that I would want to marry.

Anne's story: How I almost got married for all the wrong reasons

It was time for a new job. This became crystal clear as I was struggling to duct-tape Miss Budweiser's breasts. After her breasts were good and smashed, I sprayed her with baby oil — to make sure she was sticky, gooey, and glowing for our annual poster. The photographer kept screaming, "Spray her more!"

I know every red-blooded male in America would have switched places with me in a heartbeat. But I was a 28-year-old heterosexual female who was not particularly enjoying this — even though our photo shoot would take us from a luxury yacht to the beach and back to the yacht club pool. They say that a bad day at the beach is better than a good day at the office. But still, as sweet and friendly as the model was, I didn't enjoy the prep work one bit. I couldn't believe I was doing this. There was not a "sexing and oiling-up poster girls" course in college. It felt wrong. I felt like a traitor to my gender.

As the marketing manager for a beer distributor, I was constantly going from special event to committee meeting to bar promotion. I enjoyed many of the perks and loved the people I met. I also really liked my crazy cast of co-workers. I was a good sport — I had to be. I went to topless bars and handed out key chains. I got my commercial driver's license and learned how to tap a keg. I could fix a regulator. I could drive our big beer trailers down to the fish house and load them with ice — while hanging on to a kicking, spewing hose. I even had my own workman's shirt with my name monogrammed over the pocket in cursive: *Anne.*

But after years of night promotions, special events, and long weekends, I was done. I wanted a new job. I was lonely. Even though the job was fun, it burned me out. Many of my friends had responsible careers and were starting to settle down and get married. Kathleen and Patti were teachers. My friend Barb was a dentist. Brigette was an accountant. Suzie was seeing the world as a flight attendant and Mel and Peggy were making a killing in their sales careers. And I was riding around in a beer truck and judging bikini contests in bars. I decided it was time to grow up and be responsible, too.

But I was responsible — I just didn't see it that way. I had my own apartment. I paid my bills on time. I had car insurance, life insurance, and health insurance. I even sent out Christmas cards. But I was traveling up and down US-1 in southern Florida going to bars every night. And I — like so many other women — believed that being grown up and responsible meant being married. So I decided, I better get married. And that's when my future fiance walked into our office.

Now, I must qualify this a bit and say that my decision to grow up and marry was not completely conscious. I didn't totally connect the dots. But my subconscious observations certainly drove my decision. I'm not sure why I overlooked the complete lack of chemistry and red flags. But while researching this book, I read something that made sense. It provided some insight as to why I pursued a relationship with a guy who was all wrong for me.

In Judith Wallerstein's book, *The Good Marriage: How and Why Love Lasts*, she explains that women often look for men who have the qualities that they lack. When I read that, it rang a bell. In my case, I believe that I was looking for a responsible grown-up. And there he was. My future fiance strode into our offices with his three-piece suit, sparkling Rolex, and Hartman briefcase. He was the white-collar business executive personified. He pulled out his Mont Blanc pen and talked numbers so efficiently and effectively that my head was spinning. (Writers are bad at math.) He had a good job and was responsible.

Perfect. I can marry him. Never mind that his personality, world view, and understanding of marriage were completely different than mine. And that's where my problems began.

It's your turn

Now comes the hard part. You must ask yourself a series of questions that will help you understand why you are getting married in the first place. Secondly, you need to take a look at whether your fiance — and your relationship with him — will give you what you need for a happy marriage. And if you are not *currently* in a relationship, it's never too early to think about the kind of marriage and man you want if you do marry. Remember those calculators we talked about in the last chapter? Have you practically and thoughtfully considered all of the important characteristics you desire in your future spouse, or in a long-term relationship? Have you thought about your vision for your married life?

Why do you want to get married?

Have you carefully considered the following:
- Are you rushing to the altar? *Why* do you want to get married?
- Will you want to marry this man six months from now?
- Do you think that everything will be "perfect" once you are actually married?
- Do you believe that your life will be instantly and magically happier once you utter your vows?
- Do you *and* your boyfriend/fiance share the same goals, beliefs, and ideals for your marriage?
- Have you even *talked* about any of this with him?

Are you under pressure?

Are you feeling pressured by any of the following:
- Do your parents think it's time for you to get married?
- Do your parents want you to marry your boyfriend of many years?
- Are your friends encouraging you to get married?
- Are your friends all getting married and you want to get married too?
- Has the age that you always planned on getting married passed you by?
- Have you been dating the same person so long that you don't want to throw it all away, or to feel like you have wasted that time?
- Is your biological clock ticking?
- Do you have it together in your work life but not in your personal life? If not, would marriage really solve this?
- Are you looking for financial security?
- Do you want to get out of your parents' house?

Can the two of you even <u>have</u> a happy marriage?

Next, let's look at the core of your relationship. Could your relationship fit the definition of happy marriage? Ask yourself the following:

- Does your boyfriend respect you?
- Do you feel authentically loved, cherished and cared for?
- Does he understand how you feel and who you are?
- Is your happiness important to him?
- Does he respond to your needs?
- Does he accept you as you are?

Those are pretty short and sweet questions, but these six elements are the key ingredients of a happy relationship. You either have them or you don't. It is that plain and simple. For whatever reason, this book found its way to you and you can now choose whether or not you want to be happily married or unhappily married.

The late Randy Pausch, professor and author of *The Last Lecture,* gave a widely viewed "last lecture" at Carnegie Mellon University. In his talk, he said he didn't get married until he was 39 because "it took me that long to find someone whose happiness was more important than mine." In front of all of these intellectuals, his wish and lesson was for them to be able to find this same kind of love. He reminded them that success in personal relationships cannot be measured in any other way. Following the speech he walked over to his wife, picked her up and gave her the tenderest kiss, then carried her off the stage. This was not for show; this was spontaneous and genuine. Call it corny, unrealistic, or a fantasy. But do you also long for this kind of relationship? A relationship where you can be real, honest, vulnerable (bloated and ugly), and still be respected, cherished, understood, and responded to appropriately. Do you have it?

Standing alone to make a wise choice in your marriage

In her book, *The Good Marriage: How and Why Love Lasts,* Judith Wallerstein talks about what is necessary to make a wise choice in marriage. She calls it the ability to "stand alone":

> To stand alone, you must feel that you have a choice and that you merit a choice, that somebody will choose you and that you will have the opportunity to choose in return. Standing alone does not just mean living in your

own apartment after college. It does mean being able to get through the night by yourself. It means not being driven by loneliness to make bad decisions about who you invite into your apartment. In my experience, many wretched marriages have resulted from the fear of being alone, even briefly. [iii]

Do you have the ability to stand alone?

Now it's time to ask yourself the following:
• Are you able to stand alone or are you held back by fear?
• Are you making bad decisions about your relationships because you don't want to be alone?
• Are you limiting yourself by remaining in a relationship that does not feel right to you?
• Do you think marriage is a way out of your current loneliness or dead-end job or personal doldrums?
• If you are engaged, do you think you are getting married for the wrong reasons? Be honest.

No one else knows the answers to these questions — only you. You must decide what you need for your life, name it, discuss it, and not give in to the external pressure to marry. Pay attention to that little voice inside of you. Listen carefully to what it has to say. That is your "true self" talking and it has your best interests at heart.

---

[i] Bobbie and Robert Wolgemuth, Mark and Susan Devries. *The Most Important Year in a Woman's Life/The Most Important Year in a Man's Life*. (Grand Rapids: Zonderman, 2003), 15.

[ii]Pamela Paul. *The Starter Marriage and the Future of Matrimony*. (New York: Villard Books, 2002), 42-43

[iii] Judith S.Wallerstein and Sandra Blakeslee, *The Good Marriage: How and Why Love Lasts* (Boston/ New York: Houghton Mifflin Company, 1995), 101.

Chapter 3

Step 3: Ignore your gut feelings

Trust yourself; you know more than you think you do.
Dr. Benjamin Spock

Gut check: are you ignoring your gut feelings?

"*Do not ignore your gut feelings!*" That is probably the most important nugget of wisdom you can take away from this book. Every single woman we interviewed admonished herself for ignoring her gut feelings. Some referred to "the little voice in my head," while others called it "intuition." But no matter what they called it, they all said they ignored it, and that's how they married the wrong guy. Keep in mind that that a gut feeling serves as an alarm, or internal warning system. When your gut reacts in response to a concern or situation, it means that this system is working properly.

In the central part of the U.S., sometimes referred to as "Tornado Alley," many municipalities have tornado sirens evenly spaced along the telephone poles. When a severe storm approaches, or a funnel cloud is spotted, the sirens sound a loud warning. It's kind of eerie, particularly in the midst of a fierce thunderstorm. When people hear this sound, they know it's time to take cover, or head to the basement. They *react*. In our hometown, the sirens are tested on the first Monday of every month at precisely 11 a.m. They can be startling, particularly on a bright and sunny day. "What's with the sirens?" we ask, and then we quickly realize it's just a test. It's comforting to know that they are working and ready to go. Well, it's the same with your gut. When it reacts, you know the system is working. The key is whether or not you are going to pay attention and head to a safe place. Whatever you choose to call these feelings, let there be no doubt that this internal warning system knows what's right for you.

Gut buster check list

You need to listen carefully to what that little voice in your head is trying to tell *you* about your significant other. Are there problems in your relationship that you do not want to face? Does your boyfriend exhibit behavior that you *know* spells trouble for your future? Are you overlooking these problems? Let's carefully consider your boyfriend's behavior and how he treats you. Let's also take a look at some other issues and indicators that must be examined before committing to someone. Why? Because they can tell you a lot about a person!

- Who does your fiance spend time with?
- Does he have any friends?
- Are there socioeconomic differences that are causing problems between the two of you?
- How much debt does he have? Can you talk to him about money?
- Does he have a support system?
- How do you feel about his relationship with his family?
- Does he respect you?
- Does he call you names?
- Does he use drugs or alcohol, pornography, or have other addictive personality traits?
- Do you feel taken care of in your relationship? Is he thoughtful?
- What's the chemistry like between the two of you?
- Do you think you are settling?
- Is there physical, sexual or emotional abuse in your relationship?

Let's take a look at this checklist in more detail:

Would your boyfriend rather spend time with his friends than with you?
If your boyfriend chooses to spend most of his time with his friends vs. time with you, this can become problematic. What is so much more appealing to him about those friends? Does your partner socialize often with his coworkers? Have you been introduced to these people, why or why not? Are they even aware that you exist? (One woman we'll hear from later discovered that her new husband had never even mentioned that he was engaged or had a fiancee to his coworkers. They were shocked to see the wedding announcement in the local paper!) You don't need to be joined at the hip, but being able to share outside friendships is important. And he should *want* to share you with the folks he spends time with. It's a fine balance of nurturing you as well as the friends.

Let's take this a step further . . . does your boyfriend have any friends?

What does it mean if your boyfriend doesn't have any friends? One of our brides told us how challenging it was to be married to a man who had virtually no friends:

> He was solely dependent on me. He never went "out with the guys" because most of his friends were female. He had no life of his own. He was such an introvert and he always resisted going to family parties.

"Birds of a feather flock together" or "you can judge a man by the company he keeps." You may have heard these sayings from your parents or teachers somewhere along the line. Does an honest man hang out with a bunch of thieves? Does an honorable man enjoy the company of cheaters? Not according to this now-divorced woman: *He didn't have many friends; in fact, his best friend was a bookie. Later on, I realized he was a compulsive gambler.* This shouldn't have come as a big surprise.

Father Pat Connor is a Catholic priest in New Jersey. He has been giving the same lecture to high school girls for over forty years. The topic: "Whom Not to Marry." One of his key tidbits of advice is to *never marry a man who has no friends*. This is an easy one to figure out. Either he has friends or he doesn't. Are his friends good guys or not?

Do you and your boyfriend have socio-economic differences that cause problems?

When Julia Roberts and Richard Gere drove off into the sunset in their limousine in *Pretty Woman*, it seemed like the perfect happily ever after. She had achieved the dream of becoming "Cinderella," but let's be real. She may have learned the proper etiquette of living an affluent lifestyle, but how would her prince have fared at her family's holiday meal?

You can see it now. He shows up in his Armani suit while the rest of the men have on their favorite '80s rock band T-shirts which also serve as napkins that catch the grease from their fried chicken dinner. He's not sure where to park his shiny silver Lexus because there are too many pick-up trucks and four-wheelers in the way. The real trouble begins when he asks for a "single malt scotch served neat" and someone offers him a hit off of the beer bong instead. They say that opposites attract; polar opposites have their work cut out for them.

There are two key issues to consider when it comes to socio-economic differences. One is money and the other is social class. Let's look at the money issue first. Do you come from a family that is financially successful? Are you used to getting what you want, when you want it? Have you thought about how this will be different when you are married? How will your fiance feel about going on family vacations that are funded by your parents? Will your lifestyle expectations change or will you still shop at Saks Fifth Avenue on a Target budget? Conversely, will it be hard to switch from a frugal lifestyle to an affluent one? How you spend money, what you choose not to spend money on, and agreement on a budget are all issues that must be explored early in a serious relationship.

Social class differences can be very difficult waters to navigate. Does blue blood flow through his family's veins while your family is blue collar? Is this a source of tension? Does his family reject you because you are not a debutante? On the flip side, does your family look down on him because he didn't grow up at the country club? We understand that there are plenty of incorrigibly rude wealthy people. And a lack of money does not translate into lack of class — we get that. However, these differences can be a major source of tension. What's most important is that you and your boyfriend can acknowledge them and talk about them. Plenty of men and women have married someone from the so-called "other side of the tracks" and been blissfully happy. The crux of the matter is whether or not you face this issue head on — as a team. If his family looks down on you, does he support you? Or does he tolerate this treatment of you? Conversely, if your family is well off, how does he handle it? Does he put them down because they are rich and call them snobs? This is something that must be addressed. You'll learn everything you need to know about his views on money and social class if you observe how he handles these issues while you are dating. Here is what one woman told us:

His family had a ton of money. They were nice to me, but I know they would have preferred that he date one of the girls from their blue-blooded circle. The real problem was that while his family had a lot of money, he really didn't. He had a hard time keeping a job. He spent plenty of time keeping up with his old friends at the country club (on his parents' dime.)

He played golf constantly and drove a Porsche, but it was all for show. I ignored the fact that he didn't have much money of his own. I was kind of blinded by the idea of marrying into this really wealthy family. He was a super-sweet guy so I just looked the other way because I didn't want to deal with it. After we were married, we moved into an apartment because we couldn't afford to buy a house. Our utilities kept getting shut off while he was mooching off his parents and hanging with his friends at one of the most exclusive country clubs in town. It was a joke. I tried to talk about it with him, but he didn't get it. I don't think he was capable of changing. He was stuck: a man-child trapped in his privileged upbringing. I got out of there before he dragged my credit down with his. I should have paid attention — he was living this way the whole time we were dating.

Does your boyfriend have a lot of debt?

Many folks today live in a world of "I want it now." While our grandparents would have never dreamed about charging items they couldn't afford, today's society seems to be digging itself into a financial hole. Financial advisors like Suze Orman will tell you that not all debt is bad debt. School loans and mortgages are considered good debt and are almost a given during certain seasons of your life. But it's important to take a look at the person you plan on sharing everything with. How much bad debt do they have? Does he have a bunch of "big boy's toys" with monthly payments? A boat or a personal watercraft? A motorcycle? Does he spend more money than he makes? Does he value money? Better yet, will he value the money that *you* bring into the marriage in the same way? Do you need to furnish a new house or apartment? Does one of you need a new car? Are you planning on taking lavish vacations every year? Does he enjoy having expensive material things that do not mean as much to you? Be honest: Is he a ticking financial time bomb that may someday have your name attached to it?

It goes without saying that you must be upfront about *your* financial situation as well so there are no surprises after the honeymoon. The bottom line is: You *must* talk money and finances before the wedding. The way he handles money now is a good indicator of how he will handle it in the future.

What kind of relationship does your boyfriend have with his family of origin?

You can tell a lot about a person by how he interacts with his family. You must understand that you likely will be treated in a similar manner. A son who really loves his mother and has a healthy relationship with his sisters most likely will have good insight and respect other women. There are other men who seemingly have yet to leave the womb.

Their mothers *still* run their lives. As one woman told us:

> *I knew he had a weird relationship with his mother, but I kept ignoring it. After we got engaged, all his friends kept asking me what his mother thought. Apparently she was always hanging around his dorm room when he was in college. At our first (of only two) Christmases, the party began at 2 p.m. at his parents' house with a big spread of food and went on until 3 a.m. in the morning. Everyone was drunk. When we tried to leave at 4 p.m. to go to my parents' house his mom was furious. She said, "Where are you going? Why can't she go by herself?" I vowed that this was going to be the last time I would go to their house for the holidays. My fiance tried to appease both of us constantly. This should have clued me in . . . I told him "Your mother does not love you . . . she is IN love with you!"*

Clearly the umbilical cord was still attached and it was a life-line that no other woman could replace. (Fathers, too, can have just as much influence or power in their relationships with their adult children.)

Family-related things for you to think about might be:

- What are the family traditions that you will be entering into and are you welcomed there?
- How does your boyfriend speak to his family? Does he speak to them at all?
- How much information about your relationship does he share with his family? Does this include things that only the two of you should be sharing?

Does your partner respect you?

Does your boyfriend treat you with respect? At the end of the day, you should feel appreciated, cared for, and genuinely loved. Are you spoken to in a way that does not offend you? You are not respected if discussions begin and end with name-calling. Do you feel like you are listened to even when you may agree to disagree? Are you even allowed to disagree with him? It will be virtually impossible to not have disagreements throughout your relationship, so the key is to fight fairly. A respectful partner ends an argument with words like, "I hear what you are saying, but that's not how I feel about it."

Another example of respect is how you are treated in front of others. Are you insulted, put down, or "thrown under the bus" in social situations? If you are allowing this behavior to be acceptable now, it will continue. If you ask him to stop certain actions, or change the way he speaks to you, does he listen? If he does, you are in good shape. If you ask for it to stop and it only gets worse, you are asking for trouble.

A few words from Jen on name-calling and profanity

Many women find their way to my couch to talk about problems in their relationships. I admire every person who walks through my door. It takes a great deal of courage to share intimate details of your life with a complete stranger. Over half of my practice involves people who are having serious problems with a significant person in their life. They show up to talk about their fears, their feelings of abandonment, the pain of "things not turning out" the way they thought they would. They want another human being to help them understand how they got to that point in the first place.

As the sessions unfold, I am always amazed at how easily many women (not all) accept being mistreated. I have spent years researching and understanding cycles of violence in abusive relationships. I know how complicated this type of situation can be. But one thing has struck me over and over: many women I have spoken to don't blink an eye when their boyfriends/spouses call them names. Really awful names like bitch, whore or rag. They think it's normal, acceptable behavior.

I want to set the record straight. It is *never, ever* alright for someone who claims to love you to call you a bitch, or worse. In turn, many of my clients are incredulous when I tell them my husband has never called me a name in the twenty-two years of our relationship. "Never?" they ask in wide-eyed amazement. NEVER! He will certainly point out when I am acting hormonal, but there is a fine line between telling you that you are acting bitchy and saying you *are* a bitch. It's a very fine line and a dangerous one.

Picture this: You come home late after a long day at work. You were also late picking the kids up from the day care (again) and you now have to pay an extra $20 to the center for your repeated tardiness. You walk in the door and your husband immediately starts to grill you about why there is no dinner on the table and how you have been wasting your time. The "fbombs" start to fly and both of you become enraged. He calls you a bitch. You take the kids to their rooms and try to escape the feelings of worthlessness that just hit you like a truck. You ask your youngest child to start getting ready for his bath and your beautiful little boy looks at you and says, "No, bitch!" (Please do not think this is an exaggeration. Children become what they see modeled before them, and this happens more often than you'd think.) You have just set the precedent for not only how you will continue to be treated but how your children are being taught to treat others. Is this the kind of life you want for yourself or your future children?

One final thought: How does it feel to be put-down day-in and day-out? Think about a bad boss or nasty teacher you may have had who criticized, insulted, or made snarky comments about you. You were miserable, right? How will it feel to live with someone who does this to you every day? It won't matter if the world tells you that you're wonderful. All you'll hear are his criticisms ringing in your ears. Don't put up with it.

Does your boyfriend use illegal or prescription drugs or drink alcohol excessively?

As stated earlier, excessive drug and alcohol use is unacceptable in a relationship. We spoke to one woman who knew of her boyfriend's cocaine use but dismissed it as just a casual habit. She told us:

When we were dating, I started to realize he was kind of a "fuck up." One night before a party he said, "I am going to do coke tonight. If you don't like it you can stay home. He later apologized and I forgave.

There is nothing casual about snorting coke. You also need to realize that if your partner is doing drugs, then he/she is most likely hanging out with other people who are using drugs. Are these the people that you want to associate with? Another good question is: How much money is being spent on pot, coke, heroin, meth, or even the case or two of beer that comes home every weekend? If you work, do you want your hard-earned money to fund this?

Take a look at how Greg Behrendt and Liz Tuccillo, the authors of the No. 1 *New York Times* bestselling (and very funny) book, *He's Just Not that Into You*, respond to a woman who is concerned about her lawyer boyfriend who smokes pot everyday:

Smoking pot makes your brain work slower, and makes you less in tune with your surroundings and more introverted. It dulls your senses and clouds and impairs your sense of reality. So, he's always stoned when he's with you. That really means he likes you more when there's less of you. You're going out with someone that doesn't enjoy you at your full levels. That's tantamount to him liking you better when you're in the other room.[i]

They offer one final bit of advice on alcohol:

Don't be fooled. Don't let the guy who's not falling down drunk and peeing in his pants get away with the fact that he is quietly, more gracefully, bombed out of his mind every single moment he's with you. It's still inebriation, it's still checking out, and it's still not good enough for you.[ii]

Addictions — more than just drugs and alcohol

Addictions can come in various shapes and sizes. Folks often will minimize the seriousness of an addict's behavior because they aren't the stereotypical gutter bum who is picking through garbage and living in a box. Addicts are not just drug users and alcoholics. Addictions to gambling, food, exercising, shopping or spending money, sex, and pornography are becoming more common.

At the center of one of today's most damaging addictions is Internet pornography. Gone are the days of husbands hiding their stash of *Playboy* magazines under the bed. As the Internet continues to stream into our workplaces and homes, the access that people have to pornography can be compared to water. It's flowing directly into your home through the "pipe" that is the World Wide Web.

In January 2006, the *Washington Post* reported that the online pornography industry was worth a whopping $2.5 billion a year. Although it remains a taboo subject, pornography is having a major impact on relationships in this country and around the world.

While researching this book, we went to an online "second thoughts" forum where we saw the pleas for help from a woman who was upset because her fiance was going to Internet porn sites. She said he logged on *several times a day* and would masturbate. His porn habit was affecting their intimate relationship and they were only having sex about once a month. He ignored her pleas to stop. Instead, he preferred the company of nameless, naked strangers on a computer screen. She asked what she should do. Guess what? Most people on the forum took *his* side! They told her that, "All guys do this," or "You're being a prude." A few people supported her, but most felt it was normal behavior and wrote that she would just have to "accept it." That is so wrong! Can you say *addiction*?   (This is also a great example of the bad advice found online — but more on that later.) If you are uncomfortable with your fiance's use of pornography, you do not have to accept it. You are not being a prude. All guys do not masturbate in front of their computer screen on a daily basis.

Would you be surprised to find pornography on your boyfriend's computer, and if you did, are you OK with that? How would he respond if you confronted him? That's the most important point of all — would he be willing to stop doing something that makes you unhappy or uncomfortable?

If you are not OK with pornography, if you do not support your boyfriend's drinking and drug habits, if you resent the fact that your boyfriend talks more to his bookie than to you, then here is what you need to be prepared for. Three women who dealt with addictions of one kind or another told us:

• *He was lazy, frequently without a job. And he gambled. It wasn't until after I left him that I found out to what extent.*

• *After I filed for divorce, I found out that we owned a race horse.*

• *When we were dating he was always a big party boy; but after we got married, I found out that he smoked pot every single day.*

Addictions are always destructive and they come with baggage that goes much deeper than just bad judgment. More often than not, addictive behaviors show up in response to an often darker and hidden issue. It could be the burden of addictions in one's family of origin. Those of you who are

Irish know what we are talking about here. It could be the brain's chemical response to depression. Typically however, addictions step in as a response to some sort of trauma; be it physical, sexual, or emotional. What you might be viewing as maybe just a carry-on piece of emotional baggage is actually a U-Haul truck full to the brim. Good luck trying to unpack that truck! The good news is that people can lead successful lives and relationships if they get help for their issues. But it is a long road to recovery and you'd better be prepared to go the distance.

How do you know?

Next, let's take a closer look at how you feel about the relationship. Take a moment and think about the following questions:

Do you feel nurtured and cared for in your relationship?
Nurturing can mean different things to different people. What do *you* need to feel cared for? You might need more physical touching, such as a hug or a kiss. You might need more time to yourself in order to reenergize. Does your significant other ever do thoughtful things for you for no reason and without any expectations? And no, this does not include birthdays, anniversaries, or holidays. Sending you flowers does not count. Any fool with a telephone and a credit card can send flowers. Actions speak louder than flowers and words. A divorced woman we interviewed told us:

> *He always sent me flowers. Big, over-the-top bouquets were sent to my office. Very showy. All the ladies I worked with were jealous. Our relationship was terrible, though.*

Thoughtfulness should be spontaneous and can be as simple as bringing you your favorite cup of hot tea when you are feeling under the weather, filling up your tank with gas, or starting your car in cold weather. It may be hard to look so far ahead into the future, but you must! How will your partner respond when you are feeling sick? Will he help out when you are caring for a sick or aging parent? Will he participate in activities that he knows are important to you even if they hold no interest for him? Flowers are *easy*.

Will he cut your dad's grass every week if your father can't? Will he take care of the house and kids when you have to go away for two weeks to help your sister on bedrest with a difficult pregnancy? You already know the answer to these hypothetical questions, don't you? If he is unwilling to be thoughtful during your courtship do you really think he is going to be thoughtful 15 years into your married life? No — trust us.

Is your relationship lacking chemistry?

You also must consider the issue of chemistry. There is truth to "chemistry" being a vital part of any relationship. While we caution you about becoming blinded by the fireworks or those butterflies in your stomach, a happy, lasting relationship requires chemistry.

Think about it. When you make a new friend (of either gender) on the job, at school, or through other friends, there is chemistry at work. It influences whether you connect with that person. You laugh at the same things, share the same values, and expect certain standards in how you treat one another. You may be introduced to another person and have a lot in common, but if there is no chemistry, the potential friendship goes nowhere. Don't underestimate chemistry — it's important. Your attraction to your spouse is a well that you can draw upon when times are tough. It's a touchstone where you can find that little spark or flame of attraction that drew you together in the first place.

One woman who canceled her wedding told us:

I had to sort of force myself to be attracted to him. He was a really nice man — a decent person. But I just didn't have that spark. I kept trying to convince myself that it would come in time — or that we didn't need it to have a successful relationship. But I knew deep down I was kidding myself. I ultimately canceled the wedding because I knew there was no way our marriage would work. This wasn't the only reason; but it played a big part in my decision. I have been happily married for over ten years now and I am still attracted to my husband. Don't get me wrong, my heart doesn't race every time he walks into the room, but there is an undeniable chemistry between us. When he aggravates me or I am feeling a little bored, I think back to the beginning of our relationship and I think about how attracted we were; how crazy we were for each other. It brings all those feelings back to me.

Do you have chemistry? It's important to face this issue. Do you feel like you are more attracted to him than he is to you? Or is he more attracted to you than you are to him? You know the answer. Don't settle for a relationship with no spark or passion. In the long run, how do you think you will feel when you realize that your husband is only turned on by six-foot-tall blondes and you are a five-foot-tall brunette?

Would you describe your relationship as fulfilling?

It is vitally important to make sure that your relationship fulfills you. We know there are no perfect relationships, but if you are committing yourself to a monogamous, life-long, partnership you need to be sure that it will stand the test of time. He needs to add to your life — not subtract from it. As Judith Wallerstein says, a good marriage should be transformative. Will your relationship transform you in a positive way — or impact you in a negative way?

Do you feel like you are settling on this relationship?

Webster defines settling as the following: *to sink gradually to the bottom.* No one should ever *settle* on anything be it a job, a friendship, or a marriage. It's like a scene from the movie *Titanic.* The ship (you) hits the iceberg (settling for a poor relationship) and it seems like everything is going to be OK. There doesn't seem to be that much damage. But meanwhile, underneath the surface, there is a gaping hole that ultimately breaks you in half and *gradually* sends you into a dark abyss. Sounds pretty devastating when you think about it this way, doesn't it?

People settle for so many different reasons. Many of the reasons we heard included:

• *I didn't think anything better was going to come along.*
• *I wasn't getting any younger.*
• *My biological clock was ticking.*
• *Other people were counting on me.*
• *It seemed like a good financial decision.*

One woman told us:

> *From the beginning I felt like I was settling for something less. He was pretty short. Most people would not find him attractive. He was a smoker and this really turned me off. But I was never embarrassed to be seen with him and I think it was because of his local, pseudo-celebrity status. He was a radio personality who had been on the airwaves for years. Eventually I began to compare us to Sonny and Cher. He was the short, unattractive, and older Sonny to my taller, younger, and more attractive Cher!*

Settling into a marriage should not be an option. Settling implies two people co-habitating, without much interest in the other. That's not what the institution of marriage should be. Marriage is a partnership. It should feel like a safe place to land at the end of a long day. The security of a warm blanket that holds you close. The best part is when the blanket becomes torn and worn after years of use and it still feels as good as the day you got it, maybe even better. How safe and warm is your blanket? Do you even have one at all?

Abuse
We want to emphatically state that abuse is unacceptable in any form!

Is your boyfriend physically, verbally, or emotionally abusive towards you and/or others?

Has your boyfriend ever hit, pushed, shoved, slapped, kicked, pulled your hair, spit on you, punched, tortured, or threatened to hurt you in any way? Has he called you obscene names like whore or bitch? If so, it is time to run — not walk — back down the aisle. People in abusive relationships will tell you that repeated emotional abuse, day in and day out, can be as lethal as the pain brought on by physical abuse. Two people who truly care and respect each other do not demean, belittle, or humiliate each other. Yes, couples get annoyed, frustrated, and angry with one another. It is the way those emotions are communicated and processed that will make or break a relationship. Do you think your boyfriend has an anger management issue? How about your anger? Unless you and your boyfriend are actively seeking help for these problems, you are not safe and you are putting yourself at risk of serious mental and physical harm. No one deserves to be treated this way and it will not stop or get better after the wedding ceremony.

And finally, a word about compatibility

We know we keep repeating ourselves, but we are going to say it again. **There does not need to be any "drama" in order for a relationship to be wrong for you — you're simply incompatible. For example:**

- *One person is very social; the other person is not.*
- *One person is shy and likes to stay close to home; the other is outgoing and never misses a party.*
- *One person is deeply Catholic; the other is devoted to the Jewish faith.*
- *One wants to live in the country; the other wants to live in the city.*
- *One wants to have children; the other one doesn't.*

Three women told us:

- *He was such an introvert and I was the complete opposite.*
- *He had no male friends — all of his friends were female. I felt that he was completely dependent on me and had no life of his own.*
- *Our living style was not compatible — he was a neat freak. I completely underestimated the importance of compatibility.*

It's not fair to point the finger and say one person is at fault for the inadequacy of the relationship. It does not have to be anyone's fault; you just may be incompatible.

So what does your gut tell you to do?

After working through these questions, how do you feel? Have those nagging doubts about your boyfriend or fiance been validated? Are you facing up to what you've known all along? Should you stay or should you go? Listening to your gut will unlock hidden courage, remove obstacles, and bring out the best of your self. What is that voice saying?

- *I know we are wrong for each other.*
- *I know I need to end this but I don't want to be alone.*
- *I have lost all perception of who I am.*
- *I am too scared to even start thinking about all of this.*
- *I am making decisions from a position of weakness rather than strength.*
- *I am not feeling strong enough to do anything about my situation; I need to find that strength.*
- *I am at a crossroads in my relationship and I need to take care of myself.*
- *I have doubts about him and our relationship.*
- *I am making a mistake.*

The issues and questions in this chapter were designed to raise the issue of "red flags." The next chapter is jam-packed with real-life red flag stories as told by the women who ignored them. They all knew that their relationships were wrong; but they didn't do anything about it. **They share their stories in the hope that you *will*.**

---

[i] Greg Behrendt and Liz Tuccillo. *He's Just Not That Into You: The No-Excuses Truth to Understanding Guys* (New York: Simon Spotlight Entertainment, 2004), 73.

[ii] Behrendt and Tuccillo, 2004, p.73

Chapter 4

Step 4: Ignore all the red flags

Caution is the eldest child of wisdom.
Victor Hugo

What are red flags?

One way to practically guarantee that you will marry the wrong man is to ignore any patterns of bad behaviors — red flags — he exhibits while you are dating. What are red flags? The term comes from the use of red flags in real life. A red flag or red light on a railroad means to stop immediately. Red flags are also flown to alert people of potential danger or peril. A red flag flown by the armed forces indicates live-fire exercises. Red flags on a beach indicate dangerous water conditions and a hurricane warning is two red flags. They are indicators that should make you stop and take notice. Go no further. Pay attention: danger ahead.

Red flags in relationships are seriously unappealing or problematic actions, attitudes, and behaviors exhibited by your partner. These red flags warn you of potential problems. They are clues to future behavior; ignore them at your own peril.

Red flags in relationships

Red flags come in many forms. They can be any of the following:

• Attitudes
• Behaviors
• Actions
• Opinions

They are all useful clues that help reveal a person's character. They are also good indicators of compatibility. These clues are a way to look into the future and see what kind of a husband, father, in-law, neighbor, and co-worker he will be

One of our favorite quotes says, *"The best way to judge a person's character is how they behave when they think no one else is watching."* Little actions – both good and bad – mean a lot. They can add up to big red warning flags or uncover a really sweet guy. How true.

Anne's story: My Dad's character

My mom knew a good thing when she saw it. My dad is a real sweetheart. He is an honest, sensitive, and caring man. It's not hard to see what kind of person he is — his actions always show it. Little things mean a lot.

As a child I can clearly remember my dad driving all the way back to the grocery store after the clerk had given him too much change. It was no more than $2, but he knew the clerk had made a mistake and would be charged for it. It was not his money, so he drove all the way back to the store and returned it. That really made an impression on me. It was a small deed but a large indicator of my father's character.

Another way my father shows his character is in the way he honors his family obligations. My mother passed away a few years ago, but my dad still looks after my aunts — my mother's sisters. One of her sisters is disabled. My dad helps supervise her care. He makes sure she keeps busy and all is well in her apartment. He has her over for dinner. He helps pay her bills and does her taxes.

Recently this same aunt decided to attend her high school reunion. My dad was concerned about her so he said he would be her date. He gave up his Saturday night and dressed up in his spiffy blue blazer and a tie and escorted her to the reunion. He was afraid she would be uncomfortable and would want him to be close by. She ended up having a great time, but he was worried about her. That's the kind of man you want to marry. You want to marry the guy that will take your disabled sister to her high school reunion even after you are gone.

Chivalry is not dead

Chivalry is not dead; it just needs to be redefined. Some women may take offense if a man holds the door open for them. This may or may not be your definition of chivalry, but this type of thoughtful action is not only kind, but it's often a big help (particularly when you have your hands full). One bride told us:

I went skiing with my husband and my sister and brother-in-law. My brother-in-law carried both pairs of skis. It never dawned on my husband to carry my skis.

The bottom line is this: Is your boyfriend considerate and polite? That's what really matters. Think about these other examples of "doing the right thing." Can you even imagine your boyfriend doing the small things — the little courtesies?

- Donating blood
- Volunteering
- Shoveling a neighbor's snow-covered driveway

- Visiting with a sick neighbor or friend
- Helping out a relative (yours or his) just because
- Recognizing a need and stepping up to fill it because it is the right thing to do
- Cutting the neighbors' grass while they are on vacation, even though they did not ask
- Filling up your tank with gas when it's running low
- Grabbing a pint of your favorite ice cream
- Cleaning up the house because he knows you are overwhelmed at work
- Donating anonymously to a charity or a person in need

Don't ignore these red flags

People give us clues every day about their character — both good and bad. We've talked about some indicators of good behavior. Now let's talk about the bad. These actions and behaviors give you a big clue about what your courtship or married life will look like (unhappy). Let's say you are dating someone who has a very short fuse. He is quick to anger and easily irritated. He is argumentative and constantly getting into heated discussions with the store clerk, the gas attendant, and the waiter . . . or worse yet, your relatives. This is a big red flag. What kind of a father do you think this person would be? Children can test anyone's patience. How do you think he would handle a dinner table filled with noisy toddlers? Or what kind of employee would he be? Would he have difficulty holding on to a job or getting along with his colleagues? Is your future social life already in jeopardy because no one will want to invite *Mr. Volatility* to their parties?

We asked our brides to tell us about the red flags they observed (and subsequently ignored) in their relationships.

He lived with his mom. She would always pick up after him. Several times I witnessed him stripping naked — totally naked and watching TV. His mom would walk in on him like that. Very strange.

He wet the bed! (I think it was from drinking too much.)

*Every so often when we were having sex, he would sort of force things on me —
unexpected things. He would just do it, with no warning.*

*He was sweet but so irresponsible. He forgot to bring his license to the closing
when we bought our house. When he left to go home and get it, he ran out of gas!*

*He had a "poor" mentality. He never wanted to eat out. He ate very simply: cans
of tuna, right out of the can. (He could have afforded to eat out if he wanted to.)*

He was very competitive with me.

*I was his only friend. His dependence on me alone was exhausting. It was very
stressful to be his only friend.*

*He exhibited an explosive anger; I would describe it like a tiger coming out or a
laser beam of anger. It was not physical — but so opposite of normal behavior.
I would always cry because I was so taken aback by it.*

*One New Year's Eve, I was expecting an engagement ring. I got no ring and he
gave me a cursory kiss at midnight and then ran off to call his mother.*

*The major red flag for me was that he never wanted to make decisions regard-
ing the marriage. His responses were always, "I am really stressed out because of
work right now. Can we talk about it later?" At first this didn't bother me because he did, in fact, have a very stressful job. However, even when he seemed re-
laxed, as soon as the word "marriage" came up, he was suddenly stressed out from
work again and became defensive and argumentative. Work was his cure-all ex-
cuse.*

*He had poor hygiene. He never brushed his teeth. After we were married he had
to get all his teeth pulled because they were rotten — he had a full set of dentures.*

He was a workaholic and in a miserable mood every Sunday night.

*He was totally dependent on me. He never went out with the guys and had no
life of his own.*

He got his feelings hurt so easily. He would be wounded by any comment he perceived as the slightest criticism. It was tiring.

He partied like a rock star. He was living with his parents but crashing at my place. When we had our first fight he was screaming, "Fuck you!" Even as I left for work, he kept screaming at me. Alarms were going off inside me, but I was madly in love. My maternal instincts kicked in — I empathized and thought I could fix him. He was verbally abusive. He called me terrible, obscene words. I was always walking on eggshells. We had fights, turmoil all the time. Anything could trip his switch . . . if I took too long in the bathroom or told him to hurry up. His family was the same. His mom was always walking on eggshells around his dad. His mom put up with all this crap. He was loaded up with issues.

He had one fatal flaw which affected everything about our life together — he was a pathological liar. He said he had a college degree and didn't. He lied about a big inheritance — then said his mom stole it. He lied to impress people with his intellect or wealth. He didn't pay bills. He would lie, and then get some kind of thrill over seeing how long he could get away with it.

He was conceited and very full of himself. He tried to make me feel guilty because my parents had a lot of money and his parents didn't. He was not friendly to everybody — only those from whom he could benefit financially or socially. He always wanted to do what he wanted to do — never what I wanted to do. He always wanted to be in a group setting and never one-on-one with me. He was verbally abusive and would play head games with me. He would say things, and then when I would get upset about it he would tell me I imagined them. He also constantly lied. He visited me in college once with hickies on his neck and told me that I was the only one he was dating. He also hit on girls in front of me all the time. He put his mother and guy friends first, before me. He never complimented me on anything I did.

He ignored me. He would listen to the radio, watch TV, and read the newspaper all at the same time.

He would stand me up or be four hours late for dates — with no apologies or explanation.

We did not have a good physical relationship. He always had to watch porn before we had sex.

He was very demanding and short-tempered.

He had been married three times!

He was very materialistic and self-centered. He cared about things, not people.

He had no drive or desire for self-improvement.

He called himself "brutally honest," to the point where I would get embarrassed by the things he said in front of other people. He usually came off as arrogant when he explained that he was "brutally honest." He was always encouraging me to be confrontational with people and criticizing me for finding other ways to resolve conflict.

He constantly pointed out my shortcomings. The longer we were together, the bolder and more demanding his observations became. Soon, my long hair had to go so that I would look more grown up. I needed to get rid of my "hippie" clothes and dress more "reasonably." My shoes were not dressy enough. I needed to get a different coat. Then I was told that my laugh was too loud, that I opened my mouth too much when I laughed, that I shouldn't hang around with my hippie sister so much, that my family had one inadequacy after another, etc. I was told how to look and behave; nothing I did was adequate. All I wanted to do was please him and make him happy, so I kept buying into his and his family's assessments of my inadequacies.

He was not even employed when we met. He held a grudge against my parents for kicking me out of their home when I had already forgiven them and moved on. When we argued he would take my keys, or pull spark plugs from the car so I would not leave. I was a very social person and he was not. He would get angry that I wanted to go out with my friends. He would make me feel so guilty about wanting to spend time with them, "and not with him."

He didn't trust me. He could get very jealous and in my job, I was primarily teaching or working with other men. At first I judged the jealousy as love. I remember on our wedding night I danced non-stop with my new husband, as well as many cousins and close male friends and family. That night, he revealed to me that he was very angry because I had "ignored" him all night. He never forgave me for this and reminded me of it for the next few years.

He was always belittling me and lying to me. I was from a very close family and noticed that his family was not cohesive. They would come for family events, arrive, sit down, eat, and leave. Everyone was just going through the motions. His dad was very belittling — there was underlying sarcasm in everything he said.

When we were dating his car was stolen. He then told me he arranged to have it stolen to collect the insurance money. He smoked and lied about it. He was manipulative and did not keep his promises. He also lied about graduating from college. He got a job that did not require proof, or a transcript from graduation. He lied to his employers.

My fiance didn't have a life outside of me. He revolved <u>everything</u> around me. He didn't have many friends . . . and he would never make plans with those that he had. I guess you could say he didn't have his own life. <u>I</u> was his life.

He greatly needed his parents' approval, particularly his father's.

I am a very outgoing person. My family always joked with me when I was little and said I could make friends with anyone. I almost always have a smile on my face, I have an optimistic attitude and I am very independent. My fiance, on the other hand, was not at all like me. He was very reserved and shy, never cracked a smile, and just in general never seemed like he was happy. Friends of mine even called him the mortuary worker after we broke up because he was so stone-faced all of the time.

He was an only child and his mother always made me feel like I was not good enough for her son. It is hard to be around someone who makes you feel that way. His mother and father divorced when he was young and his mother had hatred toward his father. After my fiance and I were engaged, she met a man and became engaged and it was almost like she was "keeping up with us." Her ring had to be bigger than mine; her house had to be newer than ours, etc. It was never like she could just be happy for my fiance and I; it was like she had to beat us at everything.

My fiance had been cheated on by past girlfriends and so he was always questioning my actions. At that point in my life, I was working full-time and going to college in the evenings, I barely had time for myself. Living under a microscope is never fun and if you do not have trust in a relationship, it is bound for failure.

It felt like I was another item to be checked off his "Life To-Do List" instead of someone he loved. He was at the point that it was time for him to say he had a wife, and he had to have a son (I was in my twenties so it was assumed I would be able to produce an heir – turns out that would not have been the case). He had gone to college in the Midwest and knew that he wanted a Midwestern wife because she would work hard and not demand too much from him.

He was always getting caught in lies but was a smooth talker, so he was able to make you second-guess yourself and the people who you believed in. He would show his temper more and more over time and then shower me with "I'm sorrys" and flowers. Kind of a knock-you-down-then-pick-you-up relationship. It started slowly and built up over time.

Red flags are patterns of behavior

We understand that everyone has their bad days. All of us have snapped at a store clerk or gotten testy with a coworker . . . and then regretted it and hopefully apologized. True red flags indicate an *ongoing* pattern of behavior. You don't have to be a psychologist to figure out whether or not your boyfriend has anger issues or has a problem holding a job. The key is whether you are willing to see these red flags for what they are . . . and for what they mean for your future.

The other kind of red flags — how you are feeling?

We also need to talk about *your own* feelings and behaviors that may signal trouble. They serve as warnings that you are making a mistake. How are you behaving? Do you feel sick or uneasy? Have you lowered your standards in order to keep this relationship or planned wedding on track? What red flags are flying in your own mind about your relationship or upcoming wedding? Consider the following questions:

Do you allow your boyfriend to treat you differently than your friends treat you?
Think about your friends for a minute. It is interesting how women and men are willing to tolerate poor behavior or boredom in their romantic relationships but are unwilling to do so in their friendships. What would you do if a friend did the following?

• Was inconsiderate of your feelings
• Did not honor special occasions such as your birthday with a card or a phone call
• Did not return phone calls
• Lied to you
• Belittled you
• Bored you
• Did not share the same sense of humor
• Spoke disrespectfully to you
• Drank too much
• Refused to see the movies you wanted to see
• Avoided socializing with your family
• Preferred the company of other friends to yours
• Did not make an effort to be spend time with you

If a girlfriend treated you poorly, you would eventually drop her. Why would you tolerate this kind of treatment from your boyfriend? It is unfortunate how we seem to set the bar higher for our friendships than our romantic relationships. Many times we are willing to make excuses or justify bad behavior in our partners just to keep the relationship moving forward. Our standards should remain the same for our friends and our partners. Are you setting the bar lower for your boyfriend? That's a big red flag!

One woman listed all of the following red flags that she observed in her relationship:

He invited me to move in right away — but it was more for practical reasons.
He did not like sex much — he was very negative about it.
He wanted a "mom" around to clean up and cook for him.
He had a terrible temper and lots of rage.
His family was very dysfunctional. His mother was divorced four times, one sister never lived far away and never came home, the other sister very unhappy and cheating on her husband (this was the sister to whom he was closest to).
He had lots of acquaintances, but no real close friends at all.
He jokingly called me "bitch," saying "beeyaatch" even when I asked him to stop.
He would yell at me and I would yell back.

Why would you sign up for a lifetime of this? What was he like after they got married? (*Hint: He wanted a mom, he was rude, he was a yeller, they never had sex, his family drove her crazy, and he had no social life. It was a bad marriage and they got divorced.*)

Have you isolated yourself from your friends and family since you met your boyfriend?

Many of the people we spoke to stated that as their relationship got more and more serious, they lost connection with their close friends and family members. Some were even encouraged by their boyfriend to do so. Comments like, "You don't need them — you have me now" is like an invitation to abandon the people we love and care for. A few brides' isolation from family and friends was self-inflicted. They couldn't face them in the midst of their doubt and shame about their soon-to-be-mistaken wedding. This makes perfect sense. If you are lying to everyone you know about a wedding that you are dreading, there's a good chance that you will want to avoid everything and everyone associated with it. One woman shares some signs she ignored as her fiance tried to drive a wedge between her and her family:

Looking back I can see some red flags that I should have taken note of. He was very rude and disrespectful to his mother and other women in his family. He has no sisters and his mom was the only female role model growing up. He and his brothers would pick on his mom and she would allow them to speak to her that way. He often commented on her weight, how she cooked, cleaned, and treated his father. His dad usually just laughed and encouraged the behavior. Another red flag is that he often disrespected my family members. Not to their faces, but he always talked bad about them to me. Even though he knew how important my family was to me, it was like he was turning me against them by always pointing out their negative characteristics and things they did that he did not approve of.

When you think about getting married, do you experience an extreme reaction in your body?

Do you get chronic headaches, grit your teeth, or have other, unexplainable symptoms like aches and pains, or irritable bowels? Very often our stress manifests itself as physical symptoms. These are often referred to as "somatic complaints." Yes, you really do feel the pain, but there is not anything medically wrong with you. So even when your brain tells you that you have "everything under control," your body knows the truth. That stress and emotional turmoil can manifest itself through serious depression or severe anxiety. Traditional medicine once frowned on a more holistic approach to health. Today, many physicians understand the mind-body connection and are encouraging their patients to meditate, practice yoga, and pay better attention to how their mood affects their overall health. Unfortunately, most of us don't take the time to really understand what our bodies are trying to tell us.

Take notice of your body right now. How are you breathing? If your breath is shallow and brief, try slowing it down. How do you feel now? Do you notice any tightness, irritation, or pain anywhere in your body? If you do, pay attention to that discomfort and find out a little more about it. Many times, people will carry stress in their neck, shoulders, lower back, or their head. Others may have cramping in their stomach. Find out where you carry your burdens and start to take care of yourself. More importantly, you need to evaluate whether or not your reservations and concerns about your relationship are causing physiological symptoms. If so, it is time to pay careful attention to what your body and mind are trying to tell you. If you are wishfully thinking that these thoughts and feelings, aches and pains will disappear after the big day, we are sorry to tell you that they will probably only get worse.

Anne's story: How Burger King helped me see the red flags.

"Can I order a margarita?" I knew before these words were out of my mouth that I was losing my mind. I was actually asking my fiance's permission to order a frozen drink. My sister, in town for a visit, about fell out of her chair. She could not believe that her bossy, dominating, and loud big sister (me) was seeking permission for a margarita. Yes, it's true. After just a few weeks of unemployment, job hunting, and subtle put-downs from my fiance I was starting to crack up. (And I don't mean laugh.)

I didn't want to move up to Chicago without a job, but due to the high price of airline tickets and the hassle factor, we decided that I would relocate. Not smart. I knew better. (Don't ever quit your old job without securing a new one!) But I told myself I had a nice resume and impressive job experience. Remember, I could duct-tape and oil up a poster girl in two minutes flat! But here I was, starting to deteriorate after just a few weeks.

I have heard people wonder why abused women don't "just leave," but it is so much more complicated than that. Earlier that week, I had gone on a 7 a.m. job interview at a radio station. When I was finished, I ran across the street and grabbed an egg and cheese bagel from Burger King. I polished off my 99-cent sandwich and didn't think twice when I threw the Burger King bag in the trash can in his kitchen. Later that night he asked about it. "Well you sure are spending a lot of money dining out for someone who is unemployed," he told me. Inwardly, I rolled my eyes, but I didn't defend myself to him.

Two days later, I returned for a second interview. Back to Burger King I went for another yummy sandwich. This time, however, I carefully disposed of the evidence before I got home. I realized that this was highly dysfunctional behavior. I was hiding this from him because I knew he would put me down if he saw another Burger King bag. I couldn't believe myself. Just like that, I was starting to walk on eggshells around him.

Later that week, he told me I was using too much toilet paper. What? It dawned on me that on a very subtle level, I was starting to change. I think it was the combination of unemployment, living in an unfamiliar town, and the dawning realization that I was in the wrong relationship. I felt trapped and weak. My self esteem was starting to drain out of me like air from a limp balloon. The good news was that my inner self was starting to take control and warn me about the changes in my behavior. I was aware of it. And sometimes that's all you need — awareness. And now, every time I eat an egg and cheese bagel from Burger King, I feel empowered!

Are you actively involved in your wedding planning, or are you leaving it up to others?

Many brides might say that at some point the wedding planning process is overwhelming torture. However, whether you are planning a simple ceremony or a destination extravaganza, the ultimate goal is to cross the finish line with that one true person who you choose to share your life with. So why are you not actively involved with the wedding planning? Is your boyfriend bullying you into making decisions? Worse, is your boyfriend's family bullying you into making decisions that you disagree with? Is your wedding meeting the needs of everyone else in your life, like your mother and father who got married by the justice of the peace and are now living vicariously through you? Are you praying that a hurricane will come through and carry you off to a deserted island, away from all this madness? As one woman who ended up calling off her wedding told us:

My unwillingness to fully engage in the wedding planning process was a red flag to me. If you knew me, you would know that I am an "uber-organizer" (just ask those who were in my <u>real</u> wedding). But for this one, I just couldn't seem to get things done. I had us do a fourteen-month engagement for no real reason other than I felt that I should not rush into the wedding despite the fact that we had dated for three years at the point of our engagement.

Are you drinking or using drugs (prescription or illegal) to ease your stress?

Drug and alcohol use is one of the easiest ways you can escape your feelings. The women on *Sex and the City* were masters at resolving their issues over a couple of cosmopolitans. Unfortunately, your problems will still be there waiting for you after you cure your hangover. Not to mention the many mistakes we all make when our judgment is clouded by vodka and cranberry juice.

How well are you sleeping at night? Are you in the habit of taking a few Valium from your mother's medicine cabinet to help you catch some z's? Your body should naturally be able to slow down and rest when you need it to. Not getting enough sleep can make any sane person crazy, but if lack of sleep is a result of paranoia related to your upcoming nuptials, numbing yourself with drugs and alcohol is not the answer. It's also a clue that something is wrong — a red flag.

Red Flags

A series of red flags as told by someone who called it off:

My sister called and said she and her fiance were thinking about a holiday ski trip in Vermont. She was wondering whether we wanted to join them. I loved to ski — it sounded like a blast. It would be a great way to spend some time together and let the guys get to know each other. He said, "No, I don't like to ski." Just like that. A little voice in my head said, "Well, I guess you are never going to go snow skiing again." I am not sure why none of the other voices in my head spoke up and disagreed!

A great floating river meandered within a mile of our home. I suggested we go on a float trip. It could not have been easier or closer to spend a day on the river. "Nope," he said. "I don't like float trips."

When I would visit him during the time I lived out of town, all he would ever want to do is sit around his house and watch sports. In the beginning of our relationship, he would plan activities and outings. But after a while, he completely stopped. His colleagues from work — a really nice bunch of people — were always commenting about how he never wanted to go out or do anything. In fact, his boss wondered how I got him out of the house. She said: "I would imagine you'd have to light a bomb under his couch to get him up off of it." She was right.

I spent some time with his parents and I was appalled at the way his dad spoke to his mom. She was a sweetheart. I was so uncomfortable. I knew better than to ignore this – I was aware that this was an excellent indicator of their family dynamics. I could see some of this behavior in my fiance and realized I was getting a look at how he would treat me. I also observed his sister treating her husband in a similar fashion.

He didn't have a lot of friends. There was a couple he kind of hung around with from time to time. He had an old college buddy that lived in Florida. But that was about it. Why?

What did the red flags described in the preceding box really mean?

- He was inactive and did not like to leave the house.
- His lack of activity was legendary among his coworkers.
- He did not have a lot of friends — why?
- He did not have a positive parental role model for how a husband should treat his wife. I understood that I was going to be the recipient of his lack of understanding.
- He would not participate in activities that did not interest him. I better not plan on doing any activities that he did not want to do.

You too can have a marriage like this!

Have you ignored your friends' and family's suggestions that your boyfriend might not be the right person for you? Their warnings are red flags!

They say hindsight is 20/20. Put on your glasses and take a good, hard look at your relationship now. We have spoken to many women who said, *"My friends tried to warn me, but I just didn't listen."* Unless you surround yourself with a school of piranhas, your friends and family are probably looking out for your best interests. LISTEN, LISTEN, LISTEN not only to your inner voice but to the voices of the people who care about you most. If more than one friend or relative has expressed concerns about your choice in mate, the odds are pretty good that this person is not the right one for you. Three different women share their thoughts on this:

I was going to be his fourth wife. My grandfather said to me, "Three women can not be wrong!"

Two of my friends tried to intervene and tell me not to marry him. He turned it around on them — as if they were the problem. It ruined my friendships. We didn't talk again until years later, after I divorced. No one else tried to say anything after what happened with those two friends.

My friends couldn't stand him. They couldn't understand why I was with him. They used to say he had a personality like a doorknob. My friends would see him out with other girls and tell me he was cheating on me. Of course, he always had an answer when I confronted him about this.

Are you willing to take that kind of gamble with your life? Replay those conversations you have had with others about your upcoming nuptials. What kind of body language does your best friend have when you talk about your boyfriend? How many of your friends are not coming to your wedding? What is the message, verbal and nonverbal, that you are receiving from others? Deep down, you know the answer to this question. Why would your friends risk posing this question to you? They are not jealous, upset, vengeful, etc. It is not that they don't understand what a difficult childhood, home life, or amount of stress your boyfriend is enduring. By turning a deaf ear, you are denying yourself true happiness. You need to listen.

What you see now is what you get later

The most important point to take away from this chapter is this: What you see now is what you get later. A red-flag behavior *now* translates into an even more unpleasant behavior after marriage. It may change or morph into something different, but it will be worse … not better.

One woman from New York City told us:

I had a terrible flu and was dehydrated. My husband put me in a cab to the doctor's office. The staff was absolutely appalled that I had arrived in a taxi. I ended up in the hospital. I was upset and I told him that I couldn't count on him. He said to me, "If someone blew up the World Trade Center and they put a gun to your head, I would come rescue you." This was before the terrible catastrophe of September 11, 2001, but the point was that he would only do something heroic for me. He would never agree to the day-in and day-out things. I didn't want heroism. I wanted someone to count on every day for the little things. I couldn't count on him to drop everything for me."

Looking ahead: A glimpse into real married life

Here are two exercises for you. These are not farfetched scenarios—they are based on real stories.

The stomach flu scenario:

Picture this: You have the stomach flu. Two of your three children have the stomach flu. You feel and look like hell. The house is a mess. It is January and it is 12 degrees outside. You have barely slept. The baby cannot get the flu — he must stay away from you and the other two children. You need your husband to take over. People have been vomiting all night long and there are hardly any clean sheets or towels left in the house. He must do laundry and take the baby to the grocery store to buy some Gatorade, popsicles, and Pedialyte so no one gets dehydrated. You must take to your bed. This is the mission —could your current boyfriend accomplish it?

The "I need someone to recognize that I need help" scenario:

You are an accountant. It is tax season. You are exhausted. You are not eating right. The laundry is piling up. Your dog needs his shots and your car needs an oil change. Your gas tank is on empty. Will your boyfriend recognize he needs to help you out? Will he step up and head to the grocery store, clean the house, prepare a few meals and/or take the dog to the vet? Will he fill up your tank and change the oil? Or will he complain that your house looks like crap and he hasn't had a decent meal in weeks?

Take time to reflect on the red flags we've discussed and note any similarities to your current relationship. Ask yourself:

- What are the red flags in your relationship?
- What concerns you about your boyfriend or fiance?
- What are his good qualities? Are they outweighed by the red flags?
- Read the scenarios listed above—how would your boyfriend or fiance respond in these situations? Be honest!

Remember — everyone we spoke with agreed to share her story in order to spare you from making the same painful mistake she did. Listen and learn. DO NOT IGNORE THE RED FLAGS! If you do, we can practically guarantee you will end up in an unhappy marriage.

Red flags = trouble now and trouble later.

What Happens When
You MARRY
the
WRONG GUY?

Chapter 5

What to expect when you marry the wrong guy: **TRUE STORIES**

Marriage is miserable unless you find the right person that is your soul mate, and that takes a lot of looking.
Marvin Gaye

What to expect after the wedding; sadness, pain and heartache

Wouldn't it be great to have a crystal ball? A glimpse into the future might be all you need to guide your choice of a husband. Most of us wouldn't really want to see our *entire* future all at once. Events such as car accidents or illnesses are particularly scary because there's nothing we can do to stop them. The choice of husband, however, is something over which you have complete control. Our crystal ball can show you what your future marriage will look like. And in all cases here, a poor choice led to some pretty scary stuff.

Since we have no crystal ball, we offer you the next best thing: true stories. This chapter is filled with real-life tales from women who ignored the signs and refused to look into the future. Their boyfriends *gave them a glimpse* of what their future married life would be like. If only they had paid closer attention to their fiance's day-to-day behavior *before* the wedding. They ignored the ominous signs. They did not call off their weddings. They now realize that they should have.

Every woman we spoke to said she knew she was making a mistake as she walked down the aisle. So we asked them to look back and describe the moment, after they were married, when the reality of their mistake hit them. Many could pinpoint one event where it became crystal clear that their marriage was going to be a disaster. We also asked them to tell us about their married life. These stories may give you a glimpse into your own future.

When did the reality of your mistaken marriage hit you?

Put yourself in these women's shoes and picture yourself ... as you *finally* absorb the reality of your mistake. What's worse is that they could have avoided these painful mistakes altogether if they had found the courage to call it off.

For some women, the reality of the mistake sank in right away . . . on their wedding night or their honeymoon

I knew I made a mistake immediately. For our honeymoon the only thing he had to do was bring condoms — which he forgot. I got pregnant on our honeymoon.

We got in a fight on the second night of our honeymoon because he ran into people he knew and he wanted to have dinner with them. They were strangers to me and I wanted him to myself. He didn't care.

My first indication of how bad it was going to be was on the honeymoon. He seemed to pull away from me. It was much later that I really saw the truth. He apparently had already had several affairs.

I realized I had really made a mistake the day after our wedding, on our European honeymoon. We needed a little time to "come down" from all the excitement. There was just the two of us — no one else to reminisce with. We were jet-lagged. I caught a cold, got a yeast infection, and started my period all at the same time. We got in a horrible fight and were sniping at each other constantly. It was just fraught with emotion. It was very telling that it was just the two of us in the relationship — and we were not getting along on what was supposed to be a very romantic honeymoon abroad.

I knew it already . . . on my wedding day. There was something different about our wedding day — it was the most overtly hateful he had been. I was concerned because my dad and little brother helped move all the presents to the car, and they were upset that my husband didn't help. I just ignored it; I had a slight buzz on and was intent on having fun. Everyone had rooms at the hotel after the wedding and we partied until 4:30 a.m. I woke up the next day wondering what I had done. We left for our honeymoon that day. I kept telling myself, "This is comfortable — you can't question this." Our island honeymoon was almost boring . . . no affection, no "I love you," no "I care for you."
We actually talked or screamed about getting divorced on our honeymoon.

The reality of my mistake hit me on our wedding night. We drove to a nearby town for our first night together. We ate supper at a diner. The sliced tomatoes on my plate looked rotten. I didn't want to eat them. He intimidated me into eating them by saying that if I didn't, we would just get in the car and he would drive me back to my parents' house. I ate them. At the hotel, I won't even go into how ridiculous our "lovemaking" was, but afterwards, I threw up over and over. I cried and begged him to take me to a hospital. He wouldn't do it. The next day, we continued with our road trip. Already stick thin, I hardly ate or drank anything for the entire week. When we returned home, I did have to enter the hospital because of dehydration and a urinary tract infection. No one at the hospital asked how I had gotten into this condition.

I knew on our honeymoon in Las Vegas. I would go to bed and he would go to the casinos until 6 in the morning or so. I was alone, and when I got up, he was sleeping. He would sleep all day so he could go out at night again. From then on, for the 12 years I was married to him I felt like I was alone. He was only there to yell and hurt me, never a husband.

A couple of days after we had gotten married, we were traveling by car to South Carolina where we would be living for the next two years. One night I just broke into tears and said that I felt that I had made a terrible mistake and I wanted to go back home. He was very hurt and said how much he loved me and didn't want to see us not be together. I guess I felt that I was just having anxiety because it was the first time that I had been away from my family and friends. He, on the other hand, had not lived at home for several years, having been away at college and then in the military.

As soon as the wedding ceremony was over, it was evident what I was in for. We left the reception in a Volkswagen and several miles down the road I realized that my suitcase was not in the car. I had to argue with him to go back to my parents' house for the suitcase. He said, "It's a honeymoon, you can do without clothes." Starting then, I didn't want—and really avoided—sex.. That fact didn't change as the marriage went on. I just quit saying no and became the "wife-prostitute" because that was easier than arguing and enduring his subsequent pouting for days. He pushed sexual variations, including wanting to be nude *when we were alone. I used to say I am sure I was born with clothes on because I was extremely uncomfortable <u>without</u> clothes on, which would result in him lecturing me about being frigid.*

These women also figured it out pretty quickly

A few months after the wedding when I asked one of his friends if he was messing around, the friend couldn't answer the question. My husband was also very manipulative. He needed to have the upper hand, so he would put me down.

Less than one year into the marriage, he had a nervous breakdown and was diagnosed as bipolar. He'd keep me up at night fighting and then he'd sleep all day while I went to work (he worked sporadically until his diagnosis, and then he didn't work again for a while).

Within months of our wedding we started seeing a therapist.

Sometimes it takes another person to make you realize the mistake you made

The reality of my mistake hit me when I caught him having sex with one of our baby-sitters.

His girlfriend was calling our apartment and asking to speak to him, and he did —repeatedly.

On Valentine's Day I caught him e-mailing an old girlfriend and it was obvious he was not happy with me (this was 5 months after we got married). Nine months into our marriage I got tickets to an out-of-town concert. We had another couple joining us and we planned and spent money on a hotel, etc. He got angry about something minor and started yelling at me and belittling me. I never felt so small and unloved. This was the beginning of many fights, and this was when we should have gone our separate ways.

Sometimes a wake-up call is all it takes

I didn't really consciously take stock of my married life. I was doing well at work, moving up with raises and promotions. We went to a party at my friend's house and he got really drunk and passed out. Then we went to a hay ride and he passed out. It was like a switch flipped and I thought "You cannot have children with this man!"

What you have to look forward to if you get married anyway

Now let's take an even closer look into the day-to-day lives of women in mistaken marriages. It's not pretty. We've got infidelity, sexually transmitted diseases, sex with the 15-year-old baby sitter, lying, drugs, and a repossessed car. That reads just like a country- and-western song, doesn't it? Well it's not. Let's look again at our crystal ball and see what it is like to be married to the wrong guy.

This charming groom invited his girlfriend to the wedding

He would disappear for hours. He had a girlfriend. Our money started disappearing as well. He and his girlfriend were doing a lot of cocaine, which I also found out after we were married. This same girlfriend was also at our wedding! I didn't know that until a mutual friend told me after the fact. I also got a venereal disease thanks to their sex life.

You know it's bad when you see widowhood as the solution to your marital problems

We only had sex once or twice a month. He had a lot of mother issues. I started fantasizing about early widowhood! I became pregnant and he was demoted due to a messy office and tardiness. Our car got repossessed. Our bills were piling up and not getting paid. I wondered what was going on . . . women, gambling or drugs. I confronted him and he admitted his salary was cut. I was still thinking I was going to be able to stay home with the baby. How naïve! His boss had given him every opportunity to fix things, but two months later he was fired. I had to go back to work and he took care of the baby. He was as good a dad as he knew how to be. I came home one day and found him sacked out on the couch and the baby in the swing. I videotaped it. We ended up buying a business ninety miles away. He moved up there and I remained in our home and kept my job. We had a commuter marriage. I was so happy to be alone with my son.

I remember right before my wedding my fiance was going on a business trip to Puerto Rico. On a slightly-below-conscious level I remember thinking, I hope his plane crashes. That will solve all my problems. How sick is that?!

Throughout my first marriage I avoided coming home. A woman I worked with shared with me that the afternoon she came home from work and her husband's car was in the driveway (meaning he had returned from a trip early), and she wasn't happy about that, was the day she decided to get a divorce. Somewhere along the line, as I was hoping I would answer the door and there would be nice policeman there to tell me my husband was dead. You would have thought I would have known how unhappy I was!

Self-medicated, stoned, and playing video games is no way to go through life

After our wedding, he was in a lot of debt and I helped him get out of it. He was a foreman on a construction crew. He stayed in the same job; he had no ambition. He was constantly smoking pot. I wanted to help fix his problems. After two years I finally got hit by a bolt of lightning. I realized that he had cut off all his friendships and was playing video games constantly. He had no independent activities. He was self-medicating and withdrew into himself — constantly stoned. He got on Prozac. It was either rage or nothingness.

What's it like to live with a compulsive liar?

After a couple of years, we were essentially roommates. We lived like brother and sister. He had always been a liar and at this point he was really forcing my hand with the lying. He bought a truck and some guns behind my back. He lied about how he got them and what he paid. He told me he traded things for them. I told him, "You don't know what you're lying about, where truth ends and lies begin." I also had a dream to be a teacher, and he did not want me to do this. He was pulling me down. I couldn't pursue my own dream. I wondered, "Why am I living with a man who treats me so poorly?" He would hang out with people I didn't even know in our own driveway, and he kept showing up with new vehicles. I decided we should separate for a while and he readily agreed. We called it a separation, but I knew it would be over. It was just a really hard line to cross. By this time I was 26 and he was 32. I wanted to see what he would do if I left. He was developing other relationships with women, all in their early 20s. He was into cars, girls, and guns. Soon after I left, he moved a young woman who had a small child into our house. It was painful to see my home "taken over" by someone since I had never had a real home before this one. I went back there to get my things and found evidence of a young child. Pictures on the refrigerator — things like this. I went cold — I had seen all the signs. It was really the most painful time in my life. He told me about all the times he had been with her. It was awful.

You know it's bad when you catch your husband sleeping with your babysitter

Throughout our marriage he was a real jerk. He was verbally and physically abusive. When we returned from our honeymoon, the honeymoon was really over. He would not help with any of the household chores, wouldn't even pick his plate up from the table. He would go out and party with his friends when he was supposed to be home, or when he was supposed to meet up with me he would be several hours late. He had three different affairs within the 10 years of our marriage and denied them all, even when I had hard facts. He was a lazy, bald-headed, dishonest jerk who I had wasted 18 years of my life with. The final straw to my divorce was when I found out he had been sleeping with the 15-year-old babysitter for the previous two years of our marriage. I asked him to give her up because we had a two-year-old daughter. He said no.

Broke down and broke on the side of the highway — not romantic

He was in the military and we had to move across the country. We had a truck, a van and a Harley but no money for a hotel. We slept in rest stops along the way. When we were down to our last $10, he got a flat tire 20 miles from our destination. I had to stay in the truck, for hours, and, I felt rather explosive by time we were rescued. I decided to get cleaned up and took the last $10 to have dinner by myself. I went to a little steak house — there was a women's Bible study/meeting there. I felt like God was sending me encouragement, peace, and hope. Right then and there, I decided I hated the way things were going and decided to head home to determine whether this marriage was the right thing ..or not!

Cheating, drinking, lying, and unemployed; that's something Tammy Wynette would sing about

He was having a very public affair. <u>Everyone</u> was aware of it and talking about it. I could no longer pretend. There was so much else going on though. He was drinking too much, and he had had nine jobs in the 12 years we were married. He had also been unemployed several times. Life was tough even before I knew about the affair. I filed for divorce once and he came back very hard core again. He said to me: "How can you do this to our children and not give it one more try?" He always knew what to say to get me to cave. He then proceeded to have another affair with a girl 20 years younger. Then I was ready. It was a big paradigm shift for me. I truly believed I would never be divorced – that I would never do that to my children.

Even a strong, successful woman can be driven to depression in an unhappy marriage

I found myself sitting in closets just to be close to something (he refused to hold me). My family got me to a counselor and they helped me see how bad this relationship was. I learned later that he tried to make me miserable so that I would leave him. Instead, I almost had an emotional breakdown trying to become who he wanted . . . I couldn't face failure. With the help of counseling, I became stronger. I had gotten my MBA and was successful in my career. I realized he was holding me back, not professionally, but personally. I also realized we were in huge debt (the true extent was not known until during the divorce).

How to become a mother before you have kids

I definitely took a "mothering role" as I paid all of the bills, made most of the big decisions, etc. I was too strong for him and later on, I realized that I needed a partner, not a child. We had broken up at one point and when we got back together, somehow we decided to get married. We lived together for five years and were married for three. But for the last year he had moved back to Argentina and I was living in the U.S. We finally broke the marriage off when we started talking about having children and he immediately wanted to move back to Argentina to do this. This was never something we had talked about. It was shocking to me, since we had spent the past seven years together in the U.S. building a life. I moved to Argentina for a couple of months and then realized without my support group of friends and family, this was a hollow relationship.

Keeping up with the Joneses can be exhausting and expensive

I was so tired of his sarcastic humor with me and our sons. It was mean-spirited. He was obsessed with "keeping up with the Joneses." He always had conflicts with neighbors so we kept moving. He never wanted to go out and do things. He had difficulty with all of his jobs and was always blaming people. He was sort of stuck in his career. He was never going to follow a managerial track — there was just too much conflict.

Merry Christmas — your husband is sleeping with his secretary

At the office Christmas party, one of his coworkers pulled me aside and said to me. "You are a really nice person . . . I just wanted you to know that he and his secretary are fooling around." That was horrible.

The joy of your child's first birthday party spoiled by your cheating spouse

I wanted to make my marriage work; we had only been married a short time and I didn't want to seem like I failed. I suspected he was cheating. We went through counseling. He worked on his temper (not very well) and I tried to understand how not to push his buttons. I thought about leaving but then found out I was pregnant. So we stayed together. Having my son made me realize I needed to find that happy girl I used to be so that I could be a good mom. I went back to counseling by myself. Counseling helped me regain some of my self-confidence and realize it was ok to stand up for myself and my son. Being a mom showed me strength that I didn't know I had. Still, I didn't want to leave until I had hard proof that he was cheating on me. I searched for it. I checked his pager for strange numbers, smelled his shirts when he came home, checked up on him all the time. Finally, at my son's first birthday party, an acquaintance took me aside and told me she couldn't lie to me anymore. She filled me in on a time that my husband came to her house early in the morning telling her and her boyfriend that if his wife (me) asks, he spent the night at their house. She told me all about some girl he met. I was relieved. I finally had the "proof" I was looking for. I acted like nothing happened and went back to the party after I told my mom I would be moving back home. I waited about a week so he wouldn't know who said anything to me and moved out while he was at work for fear of what he would do.

No one should live with an abusive man

He abused me from the day we got married. I put up with it, because I didn't want to be a failure. He had a girlfriend. He persecuted my political and religious beliefs. I finally decided I couldn't take it anymore when I saw my son start to treat me with disrespect —the same way he had seen his father treat me.

Five years is a long time to be miserable

After five years, he was still finding fault with me and everything I did. The poor quality of my housework was a constant topic. One day, I had done my usual thorough Saturday cleaning, working my buns off. He came in and found some dust on top of one of the doors. He berated me, as usual. I'd had all I could stand and I slapped him. I had never laid a hand on another human being in anger since I was a toddler and didn't know any better. He slapped me back. Shortly after that day, my little sister came out to the farm on one of her rare visits. She was in nurse's training and practiced the active listening skills that she had learned. I cried for what seems now like three hours straight. I told her how miserable I was, how I had called Mom twice and told her how unhappy I was, but Mom had said that if I could just hang in there for five years, everything would be all right, that I would get used to it. Well, it had been over five years. Everything wasn't all right. I wasn't used to it. I told my husband that I wanted a separation. He was unhappy about that and asked me to give him another six months. I did, but things hadn't changed by the end of the six months. I talked to him again and he agreed: I was going to go stay with my parents (they didn't know this) until I got an apartment. We had everything all settled. I was packing a suitcase. He left the house. Unbeknownst to me, he went next door and told his parents and brother that I was leaving. His entire family got into their car and drove next door to our house and blocked the carport so that I couldn't get our car out (my husband was going to keep our truck). They wouldn't let me leave. They told me that I was insane. They finally threatened to call my parents. I defiantly told them to go ahead, my heart leaping with hope. Thankfully, my parents drove out to the farm and rescued me.

Twenty-eight years is even longer

I fought with my ex from the moment we were married to the divorce. I never shared that with anyone because he didn't beat me, etc. I convinced myself that there were worse things than fighting. Why I didn't heed the signs before the marriage and certainly <u>during</u> the marriage I will never quite figure out. All of our money was spent on him: cars, hobbies, lame projects, alcohol, and cigarettes. As we grew older his "family tapes" came alive. (He replayed the behaviors of the dysfunctional family he had grown up in.) We were always in serious conflict about his responses to our kids' adolescent activities. (two boys, two girls, and each two *years apart). What I allowed him to do to our children and our family was a travesty. For 28 years I looked for something else — I didn't know what — just something else. I did this by achieving degrees, buying clothes, joining organizations, and getting therapy. Fortunately, therapy and drugs have taken me a long way.*

A tale of red flags ignored: One bride's story of her courtship, marriage, and divorce

This bride was a smart, beautiful and capable woman who had a very successful and lucrative career. Here is what she told us about her relationship before the wedding:

He lived with his parents at the age of 27 with no intention of moving out. His mother issues were a huge red flag. All of his friends kept asking me, "What does his mom think?" after we got engaged. I also heard from several of his friends that his mom never left his side to the point that in college, she used to hang out in his dorm room when he wasn't even there.

His mother was crazy as a loon. This really came out when she drank. His family loved to party and most every evening fell apart once the cocktails began to flow. But his mom had problems beyond the love of the drink. We played on a co-ed softball team and he also played on the men's team. His parents showed up to almost every game with their cooler and lawn chairs. They would cheer from the sideline like he was still an 8-year-old Little Leaguer. At first, I thought it was nice that they joined us but hanging out at our softball games turned into hanging out at a pub on Friday night, and going to the wineries on Sundays.

I was in my mid-twenties; I wanted to pal around with friends our age. Going out every weekend with his parents got old quickly, especially when the drinks began to flow and my soon-to-be mother-in-law's whole persona started to change. Once she had a few drinks, she got this crazy look in her eye and began hurling all sorts of insulting comments that basically insinuated that nobody was good enough for her son! I was so tired of this behavior that I refused to drink any-more whenever we were around them. One evening at the regular "Friday night pub outing," she leaned across the table and clearly stated, "It's been so long since I saw Mr. Pee Pee." Immediately, my fiancé leaned across the table, pointed his finger at her and told her to "shut up!"

She wanted to call off her wedding, but she didn't. What stopped her?

I knew I had big problems but I thought I could get past them. All of my friends were already married and I was determined to get married . . . I was de-termined to make this work.

She was also concerned about her parents' money:

My parents were comfortable, but not affluent. They worked really hard for their money. I knew they had already spent about $4,500 on the wedding and I didn't have the heart to call it off and make them lose their money.

There were all sorts of red flags associated with the wedding festivities:

At our engagement party at my sister's house, his mom showed up with purple hair; she was already drunk. My sister had a beautiful house and his mom rolled out of the car and said, "Who do these people think they are?" She was crit-ical of the home, the affluence. My two aunts later told me that they witnessed his mom stop my future husband at the bottom of the steps and give him a bizarre kiss, not a mother-son kiss. A kiss on the mouth! At another point during the night she laughed and red wine came out her nose. At our rehearsal dinner she asked one of the groomsman to talk my fiancé out of the wedding saying it was the biggest mistake he would ever make. He said that it was not his place and immediately told my future husband and myself. She was very close to his best-man and at the wedding; someone overheard him actually call me a cunt!

This bride also talked herself into thinking that things would get better after the marriage. She told herself:

Even before the wedding I told myself I did not want to have children with him because I did not want to bring them up in that strange, alcoholic environment.

She didn't listen to that little voice that knew better, the one that wanted to call off the relationship. When did she realize the gravity of her mistake?

Two weeks after the wedding we went out to the wineries with some friends and of course we ran into his parents. His mom was showing some pictures of the wedding to their friends and I mentioned something about the best man calling me a nasty name at the wedding. After I said this, his mom blew a gasket. She said to me: "You deserve it, you are a bitch." I turned on her and said, "You have no right to say that — just as you had no right to try to break up our wedding." I knew this wasn't going to be good and I kept thinking I should flip on my video camera that was sitting next to me. I wish I would have because she twisted the entire story and stormed out telling everyone I called her a cunt! I was devastated. Two weeks into my marriage and she had turned their entire family against me.

So what happened next? She told us about her married life:

My husband was miserable about the rift between his mother and me. I did attempt to have a normal marriage but he NEVER wanted to have sex. I think it happened seven times in total during the eleven months we were married. That was fine with me because there was no way I was going to get pregnant. I did not want to have kids with him. I went through the motions of having a 30th birthday party for my husband. A group of my college friends pulled me aside and asked, "How long are you going to do this?" Eight months after our wedding, we were set to celebrate our first Christmas together. He went out to see his family (I was not welcome; in fact, I never spoke to them again after the winery incident) and he was to meet me later that afternoon at my aunt's house. He never showed up. I was really embarrassed. My cousins were teasing me. They said, "Where's your husband?" It wasn't in a mean way, but they all knew that this was very odd that he never came back from his mother's house. Eventually, I started having terrible headaches. I was convinced I had a brain tumor. I went and had an MRI. Nothing showed up. One day while driving home from a business trip, I glimpsed in the rear view mirror and saw my jaw clenched so tight . . . I had TMJ. I was a total stress case. I looked awful . . . just a monstrous physical mess. This marriage was a taking a terrible physical toll on me.

Eleven months after the wedding, she wrote him a Dear John letter and ended the relationship. Then what?

He went straight home to momma. He started getting really nasty about all of the money. I knew he was being coached by his mother. We had to split up our assets and I bought his share of the house. Instead of using the money as a down payment on another home, he moved back in with his parents and bought a sports car. He wanted to go back to school and wanted me to pay his tuition! I was furious. I threatened to raise the alcohol abuse issues in the family and his mother issues in divorce court. He walked away. I heard through the grapevine, many years later, nothing has changed. Not my problem anymore.

She endured emotional abuse from him and his family. She developed physical problems as a result of all the tension and she narrowly missed giving him half of her hard-earned assets. It would have been a lot easier to cancel the wedding in the first place. Hindsight is 20/20. She shares this painful story with you so you don't make the same mistake. If you have serious reservations about your relationship, you must take a step back and carefully evaluate what is best for you. Don't be tricked by the issues of un-planning a party. You must determine whether your gut is telling you to cancel your unstable relationship. Deal with those feelings first. After you acknowledge you need to end the relationship, you can then deal with the ins-and-outs of canceling a party.

(P.S. This bride later went on to marry a really great guy. She had a really small and beautiful wedding and has wonderful In-laws with whom she has a solid loving relationship. They are happily married and have three beautiful daughters. They have the same goals for their family life and enjoy spending time on sports, school activities, travel, and all the other fun that comes along with being a family. She says she's learned a lot from her mistake and has made sure to apply these painful lessons to her second marriage.)

What's driving your decisions: truth or fear?

These stories do not paint a pretty picture of a happy marriage. Our brides were clearly unhappy on the outside — just imagine their insides! Let's recap some of their emotions:

"I felt disgusted."
"I was fraught with emotion."
"I never felt so small or unloved."
"I was dreaming of early widowhood."
"I was afraid of being a failure."

They also talked about physical illness:

• Migraines
• TMJ (Temporal Mandibular Joint Disease)
• Yeast infection
• Urinary tract infection
• Dehydration
• Venereal disease

And finally, they talked about feelings of anxiety, depression, and a sense of emotional breakdown. Unfortunately, it is those feelings on the inside that often lead our decision- making. What we have learned is that the majority of our brides were feeling scared on the inside, yet they went down the aisle anyway. When we become anxious or scared, we are not mindful of our choices. Instead, we let our fear make the decisions for us. More often than not, these are the decisions that we regret later. Have you ever made a decision when you were *not* scared? Maybe it was a new job that you sought out. When you decided to apply for the job you felt confident, calm, clear. You probably breezed through the interview process and when it was over, you felt great! When you approach your decision making and behavior this way, you become in control of the choices you make. You honor what it is you really want in your life.

As you head into Chapter 6, take a moment to look at the following list of qualities we all have — but often lose sight of — in times of chaos. Put a check mark by those qualities that you have *not* felt or seen in yourself in a long time. According to Dick Schwartz, founder of The Center for Self Leadership, these qualities are available to us when we are in charge of our decision making. When they are absent, it is a good sign that our fear is in charge.

Qualities of Self Leadership:

Calmness: When situations heat up, are you calm, cool, and collected even in the midst of chaos? It's important to be able to speak without raising your voice, cursing, being aggressive, or hysterical. You also need to be able to listen without becoming defensive.

Curiosity: Rather than becoming triggered over someone else's actions or behavior, be thoughtful and curious about why someone else is behaving or acting a certain way. An example of curiosity might be simply asking yourself, "I wonder why he never calls to say he will be late getting home?" Then follow up with asking him that question without being accusatory.

Clarity: Make sure the lens you are looking through is not clouded or distorted. Are you absolutely certain your view is clear? Oftentimes we get lost in our own personal outlook and the distortions distract us from the reality of the situation.

Compassion: Are you coming from a place of understanding? As scared and angry as you might be, try to understand and acknowledge someone else's point of view even when tempers are flaring.

Confidence: Know who you are even when others are critical or hurtful towards you. Understand that you have strength and self awareness and that you are a good person no matter what the situation.

Creativity: Have the freedom to explore and express yourself in any way you want. Sing in the shower, paint or draw, go ride your bike! Find out what it is you like doing and don't hold back.

Courage: Stand up for what you believe in and what you want in your life.

Connectedness: Maintain relationships with those who are most important in your life. Don't cut yourself off from the world.

If you have not felt creativity or calmness or any of these other qualities in a while, it is a sign that your decisions *and* your relationship are not grounded in the truth.

You are now faced with making one of the *biggest* decisions of your life — whether or not to get married. Do you really want your *fear* to decide your fate? NO, NO, NO you don't! Like the stories you just read, you too know that you are headed for trouble. Only you can avoid the sadness, heartache and pain that is certainly in your future if you choose to marry the wrong guy. Chapter 6 spells out in glorious detail what it's like to get a divorce.

Chapter 6

What it's like to get a divorce: **MORE TRUE STORIES**

A divorce is like an amputation: you survive it, but there's less of you.

Margaret Atwood

It is much easier to end a relationship or call off your wedding than to live through a divorce

Instead of getting married again, I am going to find a man or woman I don't like and just give them a house. While the source of this quote is unclear, the meaning is not. When it's all said and done, you will end up sharing half of your assets with a person you don't like anymore. Divorce will cost you plenty. The price you pay in both dollars *and* emotional well-being will be high.

There have been countless books written about divorce, surviving divorce, helping your children through divorce, etc. We won't be redundant and tell you things that you have already heard. Instead of regurgitating conventional wisdom, the facts and figures — we want you to understand the reality. We want you to believe what we are telling you. So before we go any further, please memorize the following (we can't say it enough):

It is much easier to end a relationship or call off your wedding.

The majority of women we interviewed went on to healthy and fulfilling second marriages. They learned from their mistakes and chose more carefully. A few have not remarried and are happy and thriving as single women. A very few others went on to another mistaken marriage. While their marital outcomes are different, they all agreed on one thing: their divorce was one of the most painful experiences of their life.

Several women shared the details of their divorce. Keep in mind that every one of them knew that she was marrying the wrong guy—yet she did it anyway. In a not-so-ironic twist, they ultimately had to make the tough call to get a divorce. Do you think it would have been easier to call it off in the first place? You decide. Here is what they told us:

This woman describes the loneliness of a loveless marriage

He went out and bought two recliners . . . we did not physically touch one another when we watched TV. Our house became a mess which led to more fighting. We had not had sex in a long time. He closed off emotionally for a full year. I told him, "I don't think this is working," and he agreed. I caused him a lot of emotional pain — he had totally shut down. It was hard to end the marriage. It was hard to figure out who took what. We had to share our cats. It was hard to break ties with each other even though we did not want to be married anymore. Fortunately, he was very ethical and agreed to split everything right down the middle.

Marriage counseling and therapy won't fix a marriage that is wrong from the start

I just knew the marriage could not work. I knew that marriage counseling would not work. There was nothing to "save." I went to a convention and I shook off the shackles [of my unhappy marriage] and felt enlightened, alive, and confident. I had not felt this way in so long! I took off my ring and declared myself free. I came home and he was crying. I told him I was moving in with my parents. How could this marriage possibly work when he was either screaming at me or crying? My parents did not understand why the marriage was over. I was ashamed to tell them the real reasons I was leaving. I didn't want to tell them about his drug and drinking habits. I didn't want to talk about his anger and depression. I really didn't want to tell them that I knew the marriage was a mistake in the first place! How could an educated person like me be so dumb? I felt like my mom did not trust me; she was resentful. She was upset our marriage was breaking up. She kept asking me, "When are you going back home?" When I packed up, I had sobbing fits; I finally told my mom the truth. I was overcome with shame. I just decided: "Let's get on with this." It [the divorce] was very painful.

We slept in separate bedrooms. There was no love there. I told him I wanted a divorce. He wanted therapy. I wanted my freedom so bad! One foot was out the door. I wanted to do whatever it took to get out. He turned bitter and vindictive. He did not forward my mail after I moved out. He then steamed open a statement for some stock I had been gifted from an uncle. He demanded half of it.

Some women are willing to give up everything just to get out

I was tired of trying to be someone I wasn't. I wanted him to grow up. I left. I only took half of our belongings. I left a lot behind. I found an apartment all by myself — it was the first time in my life I was all alone. It was really, really hard. I cried for weeks. What was I crying for? I had an aching pain that I could do nothing about. I had given eight years of my life to this relationship — all for nothing. I was angry with myself for being blind to who he really was, even though it had been in front of me the whole time. I blamed myself for a lot of it — I had failed at marriage. Thank God I never had children with him. There is no fate worse than being linked to a lying, cheating man for life.

When I left, I left with the clothes on my back and my grandma's cedar chest. We split the credit card debt. He took everything else. I found out that the Rolex he gave me was knockoff! He was such a scofflaw.

I just wanted out. During our marriage, we had saved every single one of my paychecks from the jobs that I held during the times that I worked in town (about two out of the five years, I worked on the farm helping to milk cows). We had a total of $6,000 saved. The next morning, after I moved to town with my parents, I went to the bank to open an account with some of that money. He had been to the bank before it opened because he knew someone who worked there, told them that I had gone mad and would be in to take all the money if he didn't get it first. They let him have it all — he hadn't left me a dime — plus he had taken my name off of the checking account. If it weren't for my parents, I would've been destitute. We talked and he told me why he had done it and couldn't be reasoned out of it. We finally got him to listen to the church pastor, who actually stuck up for me and told him that he needed to give me half the money. But this wasn't until weeks later.

I would recommend that you really take stock of what you put in to the marriage and if you gave your all (like I did) and got nothing back except grief, you should take a stand for yourself. I felt guilty that he wasn't working when I kicked him out (back home to his parents) so I voluntarily took on all our marital debt (except the credit card that was in his name alone) and even gave him my wedding and engagement ring to pawn for cash to start his new life. Hindsight being 20/20, I shouldn't have felt guilty in the least. I did everything possible to save the marriage.

It was about two years into the marriage and my mother had died. His parents had a huge crisis — his father had had a mistress for many years and it all blew up. I realized that they had been so unhappy for so many years and that we were going to wind up like that and get divorced in the end, too. And I decided that life was too short to spend it in a horrible marriage. So I suggested divorce and it turned into a big fight and his family came over and it was a disaster. I had to agree to drop it — so I did. I waited, and a few months later I just packed a suitcase and left for work and never went back. I moved in with a girlfriend from work until the divorce was final. I was willing to walk away from it all and give up everything, furniture, house, possessions, etc. just to get out of it.

This woman felt financially and emotionally robbed — after eighteen years with the wrong guy

The divorce was a nightmare. All of our goals were broken and our dreams shattered. Everything we had built together was being divided between yours and mine. It didn't matter that I had worked two jobs to pay off his college or that my parents had given us the money for the down payment of our house. It was a battle of what the courts said was his or what was mine. The lawyers robbed us both financially and emotionally. I became a single mom and I had to start over again. I was enlightened within myself because I was not living with his abuse anymore both physically and emotionally. I actually found who I was again. When finding myself, I kept looking back at the 18 years of my life and wished I would've walked away when I had the chance.

The pain and sense of failure is hard to imagine — until it's your life and your divorce

I was so unhappy. I was such an overachiever I was ashamed to admit I was getting a divorce. I could not sleep and would take a Sominex and have a light beer every night in order to sleep. I avoided my friends. My dad finally called and said I have a lawyer for you. At that point, I realized my husband had hidden all of the assets.

How could I — a strong, independent woman let myself get into this position? I had a long haul to forgive myself. It was hard to look back and believe that was me.

I felt a lot of self-hate over the divorce. I felt like a failure. I tried to never think about it.

I realized he was holding me back, not professionally, but personally. In addition, we were in huge debt (the true extent was not known until during the divorce). I felt like I was a failure: to my family, myself, my God.

These two women found themselves in danger as their divorce proceedings moved forward

He moved his things out in a week. I got it all together and watched him leave and did not shed a tear. He served me papers. He showed up one evening and I let him in. We had a struggle over the dog. I was scared and called the police. I reported that he took the dog. I went to his family about this. He said I could have the dog. I found out from his step- mom that he had bought a gun and ammunition and was envisioning my death. I sent a friend to get the dog.

It (the divorce) was truly one of the worst experiences of my life. He stole my car, took my kids and I had no idea where they went, and tried to kill me on several occasions. I truly wish I had never let it go that far. These are things that could have been avoided if I had followed my instinct back then.

Her divorce was shadowed by regret — why didn't she just call it off in the first place?

The divorce itself was easy: no kids, no assets, file some paperwork, appear before the judge. But for me, I felt like a failure. I still feel like I failed myself. Why did I marry someone who I knew was not the love of my life and I did not have a good relationship with? I married him because we were friends. We had a great friendship at one time. That is all we had though. When it came to a relationship, we had nothing. I was determined to never divorce so I thought if I married him, our friendship would be enough. In many ways we had a friendship and a relationship of convenience. It was not enough. I still know I failed myself by not getting out when I should have (six months after living with him). I was too embarrassed by my mistake and I went through with it anyway.

She tried to make the best of it, but the truth eventually came out

It was right before our wedding anniversary and he just said, out of the blue one day, that he didn't love me anymore and that he needed to be on his own. I was in shock, and told him to leave. He went to stay with his mother. Several weeks later I discovered that he had been sexually harassing my sister for over a year and several of my girlfriends, who were also his friends, for about that same amount of time. No one had said a thing to me about any of this because they thought that it would hurt me and that maybe he was just going through some midlife crisis or that they had done something to bring on his unwanted attention. And if that wasn't devastating enough, I later found evidence that he had a girlfriend in another state. I then started the divorce proceedings. Going through a divorce is just horrible. I was very scared. It made me physically ill and I found it difficult to think clearly. I was also worried about my children and other family members and the effect that it would have on their lives. I felt a combination of feelings. I felt very guilty, that maybe I hadn't been a good-enough wife. I also couldn't understand how I could have been so stupid at not seeing what he had done.

Divorce can be worse when there are children involved

I finally decided I was done. He tried to sabotage me. He kept calling my family members. He was depressed and angry that I had a support system while he did not. He kept putting the kids in the middle. We did try counseling but he refused to go back. I felt relief and happiness it was over. It was very hard financially, but I was so much happier once I left him.

My divorce was awful — especially because we had two kids. My dad had died by the time I got divorced. I could have really used his support during this time. He was such a great guy. During my sad times during the divorce, I kept seeing rainbows. My dad had always loved rainbows and I think it was my dad's way of telling me everything was going to be ok.

'We can always get a divorce'

After talking to so many women about their divorces, two things jumped out at us. The first was the use of the term "failure" over and over again. The women were so hard on themselves. They said they never thought they would have a failed marriage. It's ironic because most of them ended up in divorce court because they didn't want to admit they had made a mistake in the first place. Such twisted logic!

The second thing was that they almost universally spoke about their divorces as one of the most painful experiences of their lives. The women felt like failures and suffered emotional pain even when *they* were the ones to initiate the divorce. We tend to believe that the spouse who walks away from the marriage suffers no ill effects. That's simply not true. Too many women convince themselves to go ahead with a mistaken marriage by using a possible divorce as their escape route. They say, "I'll just get a divorce if it doesn't work out." What they don't realize is that a divorce isn't that easy — even when you're the one who serves the papers.

Divorce is never easy. It's painful for the husband, it's painful for the wife, and it's painful for the children. Divorce affects everyone around you. Before we end this chapter, let's get another perspective on how divorce can affect grown children.

Jen's Story: an Adult Child of Divorce

I was always a very observant child. I was extremely quiet but inside I was carefully taking in everything around me. I am certain this skill led me to the career I have today as a therapist. Looking back at my early childhood, I can recall many good memories of my family. My mom's family lived within a five-mile radius of us and we were all very close. We had wonderful family traditions. Like all good Irish families we treated St. Patrick's Day like it was Christmas! However, underneath all of that was a seri-ous crisis. My parents did not get along very well. My childhood was not traumatic by any means. There was laughter in the house, my parents supported me in all my activities and there was never any doubt that I was loved. The problem was between the two of them. And it went unspoken for almost 25 years.

I remember the phone call asking me to come to my parent's house. "We need to talk to you." My father-in-law had recently died after a long battle with cancer, so my heart sank, thinking I was going to have to find the courage to go through a similar situation with one of my own parents. The news was even more shocking and heartbreaking. My parents announced that they were separating. I felt like I had been hit over the head with a skillet only it did not knock me out. I almost wish it had because I just sort of shut down at that point. My mom was crying, I could tell she was angry and hurt. My dad was also upset and tearful. He started to talk about how he had not been happy for almost 16 years, and that he was no longer in love with my mom. I can't tell you exactly what the words were; there was a loud buzzing in my ear that kept me from fully hearing what was being said.

I was 24 years old, newly married, in graduate school, really having the time of my life, and it seemed to all disappear in that one moment. The reality of everything I thought I knew no longer existed. The safety and security I felt in my family, in the home they had created for us, felt insecure and com-pletely annihilated. I do remember asking my dad why he waited so long to say something. Sixteen years is a long time to be living a lie. He said that he hoped it would change or get better, but it never did. Once my brother and I had grown up and moved out there did not seem to be anything else to hold them to-gether. I remember thinking, "Gee thanks, Dad. How noble of you." And like most good first-born care-takers, I immediately aligned myself on my mother's team. If he was not going to take care of her, then it would have to be me.

Needless to say, their divorce was not cordial. To this day my parents have not spoken more than a few words to each other, much less been in the same room together. That part is frustrating. How do you live a life with someone for 25 years and then never speak to them again? The most awful part of my parents' divorce was the day they had an estate sale to liquidate their "stuff." Furniture, books, dishes, linens, you name it. It made me sick to my stomach to think that complete strangers were picking through my life and taking small pieces of that life home with them. "Hey wait! That's mine! That belongs in the living room next to the ceramic pencil holder I made in fourth grade!" It sounds silly now, but at the time it was excruciating. Estate sales take place when someone in your family dies or even when your parents decide to downsize and move to a condo in Florida to live out their golden years. My parents were alive and well; they did not die but I was grieving in a way that I had never experienced before or since. As their home became dismantled, so did our whole family.

I have had the past 13 years to take inventory of my parents' relationship. As much as it hurts, here is the reality:

- *My parents barely knew each other when they got married. They had a long-distance courtship while my dad served in Vietnam. It may sound romantic, but that early romance did not last.*

- My mom has come to terms with the fact that she, herself, had doubts about her relationship with my dad on her wedding day. Parts of her story are sprinkled throughout this book.
- My parents fought with each other quite a bit. There was a lot of anger in those fights and I never saw them apologize to each other.
- My dad drank a lot on the weekends, probably as a way to cope with his unhappiness. My mom hated his drinking. The more she criticized him the more he drank.
- My parents did not respect their differences. It often came across as very judgmental.
- My parents rarely had dates together.
- They differed on their religious beliefs.
- They often disagreed on parenting styles and would argue about this in front of me and my brother. I do recall brief moments of them being happy together but there are not many examples.
- When I was a child, I thought that this was what a "normal" married couple did and I never questioned their behavior. This changed one day when I was a bit older, driving in the car with my mom. As we pulled into the car port, the Dan Fogelberg song, "Same Old Lang Syne," came on and my mom just started crying. If you are not familiar with this song, it is about lost love and missed opportunities. I had a "gut" feeling in that moment that something was not quite right with my parents. It was such a sad song.

Although I am now much older, wiser and more self-aware, the pain that I felt that day in my parent's living room will forever be with me. I still have a difficult time driving by the house I grew up in. The people that bought it have not taken care of it the way we did. The beautiful gardens my mom planted have become overgrown with weeds. The new owners have put a huge privacy fence around the backyard so you can no longer see in. That house has become a symbol of how my family fell apart. I went through a roller coaster of emotions following my parents' separation and divorce. At the peak of the hill was anger, then sadness, then guilt (I felt responsible in some ways for not being able to keep them together).

My parents' divorce is by far the most difficult thing I have ever dealt with and continue to deal with. I often wonder what the experience would have been like as a child. Going back and forth, splitting up holidays between two houses, not having the same financial resources. How would I have dealt with this as a child? I know as a grown, married adult, it was still upsetting. I don't blame my parents for the choices they made. They gave me life and I am grateful for that choice! I know I was conceived out of love and I know that my parents love me — and I've never felt otherwise. I share my story with you not for pity, but to bring awareness to the serious consequences of your actions. Getting married impacts everyone around you and the consequences of divorce impact everyone around you. The consequences impact your family, your friends, your children, your co-workers, your neighbors, and even your pets. That's why it's so important to remember that you can deal with all of this mess of a divorce down the road, or you can simply walk away now, while there's time.

How can you argue with the truth?

These stories spell it out pretty clearly. If there are problems with your relationship that you know are beyond repair — you must get out of the relationship. If you don't, chances are almost 100 percent that you will have a troubled, unhappy marriage. This is what will happen if you don't call off your wedding. These fearless women have shared their stories of divorce. They told us what it was like. Let's recap what we heard in our true-life divorce tales:

- Adultery
- Attempted murder
- Dog-napping
- Tears
- Hidden debt
- Sadness
- Insomnia
- Fear
- Arguments over money
- Self-blame
- Feelings of failure
- Guilt
- Sexual harassment
- Kids stuck in the middle
- Pain and anguish

Wouldn't you rather deal with a canceled wedding than any of the above?

Tears, sadness, depression

Hopefully, these stories have brought to life the depth of pain, misery, and sadness experienced by these women. You've read the real-life stories of paying off his bad debt, tears, lies, deception, guilt, and walking away with nothing — just to get away. It would have been a lot simpler to cancel the wedding. Are you ready to take our wedding pledge?

I (state your name) fully understand that it will be much easier to call off my wedding than to live through a divorce. I am also completely convinced that it is better to avoid getting married in the first place rather than living through a miserable marriage.

Guess What?
YouDON'T
have to
MARRY HIM!

Chapter 7

WITH THIS RING I THEE DREAD: *What stops people from calling it off?*

Why does it take a minute to say hello and forever to say goodbye?
Author Unknown

Why is it so hard to call off a wedding?

Why is it so hard to call off a wedding? After talking to so many women who wished they had, we uncovered the eight most common reasons why they did not. And just as we discovered earlier, these reasons were remarkably similar. Let's take another look at the reasons why they felt they had no choice but go through with it. When we evaluated their responses, they fell into the following categories:

1. Fear of letting others down; hurt feelings (friends, family, and your fiance)
1. Caught up in momentum of the wedding; it was too late to call it off
3. Fear of not finding someone else to marry — this was the one and only chance
4. Belief that the relationship would improve after the wedding
5. Time invested in the relationship
6. Fear of publicly admitting a mistake; shame, embarrassment
7. Financial concerns associated with canceling the wedding
8. Confusion about canceling a party vs. canceling a relationship.

In addition to giving so many of the same reasons for failing to cancel the wedding, they also agreed on something else. Their reasons for *not* canceling their wedding were unsound. They didn't hold water. Unfortunately they figured that out too late: after the wedding, after the unhappy marriage, after the painful divorce.

Interestingly enough, the women who *did* call off their weddings cited many of the same reasons for almost getting married. However, in the end, they decided that these reasons were not worth it. They didn't care what it what it cost them — emotionally or financially.

No. 1: Fear of letting others down: hurt feelings (friends, family, and your fiance)

I felt so guilty — I did not want to let everyone down. What is interesting is that I know that my parents would have totally supported me. All of my energy was directed at finishing school at this point, so I just went ahead with it because I couldn't deal with this particular problem at the time.

Starting at a very young age, we are taught to be kind to others and to consider their feelings. It's true that the golden rule is important. However, when you put everyone else's feelings ahead of yours, it becomes a problem — especially when it comes to canceling your wedding. People who really love you will not be angry when you tell them that your relationship and wedding are over. They may express concern or dismay, but they want you to be happy and will support you either now or later. You must remind yourself that you and you alone are the only person that will be married to your future spouse. So you need to decide whether it is right for you. His family may be upset and disappointed. They may be angry. Remember — it is *your* life and you must take charge of it. If the relationship does not feel right and your fiance does not cherish or respect you — call it off. In this case you must put *your* feelings ahead of everyone else's. As one woman who called it off told us:

I think my mom always knew that I was not truly happy with my fiance. It is that whole "mother's intuition." I think I was in that stage in my life where I just wanted to get married. My family was very supportive when I called it off. Of course, my parents lost some money on deposits that they were not too thrilled about but they would have rather me called it off than to be divorced a year later.

Another woman who wished she had canceled said:

The ironic part is my mom would have completely supported me if I had. In fact, she gave me ample opportunity to cancel the wedding. She carefully broached this subject with me in a non-threatening manner. But for some reason, I didn't listen.

Why didn't she act? If telling your family seems difficult, telling your fiance is even harder. It <u>will</u> be a difficult conversation. While the pain may be with both of you for a while, the conversation does not need to go on for hours. Think about what you want to say beforehand. Talk to someone you trust before you do it to help you choose your words carefully. Remember, the truth hurts, but the truth will also set you free from a really awful mistake. One woman who did gather up the courage to call off her wedding described the day she told her fiance it was over:

When I tried to talk to my fiance about the problems I was having with the relationship, he was so disconnected. We didn't see eye to eye. In his mind, there were no problems. And that was *the problem. His idea of what a good relationship looked like was so completely different than mine. The day I told him I was leaving he went out and cut the grass. Then he came back in and yelled at me a little bit. Then he went out and washed my car and then came back and yelled a little bit more. He told me I was ungrateful and that I had unrealistic expectations. I remember thinking, "No, it's just that I had better marital role models in my parents. You don't see how poorly your dad treats your mother."*

I left and spent the night at a hotel with my parents who had driven in from out of town to help me gather my things. I went back to his house after he had gone to work the next morning and got the rest of my stuff. I got in my car and headed for my hometown nine hours away.

I didn't hear from him for two weeks. My dad expressed dismay that he didn't even try to "woo me back." I was full blast into my new life. I got a new job within days, I leased an apartment and I was really happy. I was so relieved — I felt like the weight of the world was off my shoulders. When he finally called me he said, "Hi Honey, are you ready to come back?" He was clueless — he still didn't understand that it was over. I told him. "I really meant this—we are through. I have a new job and a year-long lease. Pack up any odds and ends you find of mine around the house and send them back to me." That was that.

That was 16 years ago and I still get a warm and fuzzy feeling thinking about leaving him. That was one of the smartest, bravest things I have ever done. It still brings a smile to my face when I talk about it. I was so glad I had the courage to call this off . . . to recognize what a huge mistake it was. Yes, it was embarrassing, but the freedom and relief far outweighed any embarrassment. I was also amazed by how many people complimented me on my bravery.

No. 2: Caught up in momentum of the wedding; it was too late to call it off

Everything was organized, the party was planned, and everyone was looking forward to the wedding. (Everyone but me that is.)

I did want to call off the wedding, but just felt swept along. I wanted to keep everyone happy.

Many women said that they were so caught up in the momentum of the wedding, that it was too late to call it off. This is simply not true. It is never too late. People incorrectly think that once the plan is in motion, it's too late to stop it.

Several women told us that they felt they had passed the point of no return once they received that first wedding gift, or attended their first shower. Wrong! Don't let your wedding gifts paralyze you. A pile of beautifully-wrapped gifts does not have the power to keep you from canceling your wedding. You don't want a set of wine glasses or a wok to dictate your future.

The organist can have her fingers poised over the keyboard and you can still pull the plug. One woman called her wedding off in the wee hours of the morning after the rehearsal dinner:

So, I hung up the phone and drove to the spa to meet my bridesmaids, some already getting their nails done. One stopped at my car and asked if I was coming in . . . I burst into tears and had to explain it was being postponed or called off. It was quite a sight when four girls ran out the door with their shoes off and toes partially painted.

It wasn't easy, but she didn't regret it. It was the right thing to do.

Anne's story: How Lady Diana helped me make up my mind and cancel my wedding

Legend has it that Princess Diana wanted to cancel her wedding to Prince Charles . . . but something stopped her. And now I understood exactly how poor Lady Di felt. I thought about this as I pulled one thick and luxurious monogrammed towel after another out of a gift box. My heart sank when I took a second look at the monogrammed his-and-her Polo robes. Picked just for me at the Ralph Lauren store in Palm Beach, this gift was very generous — and non-returnable.

I was unpacking wedding gifts at my fiance's home. They had just arrived thanks to my friend and former co-worker in Florida, who had shipped several boxes of gifts to me in Chicago. I had just moved to join my fiance and begin my job search in my new home town. The gifts were from an elaborate going away party/wedding shower held in my honor a few weeks prior.

It was a catered affair with all of my favorite foods. I received dozens of wonderful gifts. But by the time these gifts arrived, I already knew I wanted to call off the wedding. As I unpacked each gift, I felt progressively more nauseous. I thought of all the nice people who had carefully selected these presents . . . just for me. I considered all the planning that went into the party and how much fun it was. I reflected on how happy everyone seemed to be for me. I can clearly remember thinking: "It's too late to call off the wedding because the towels have already been monogrammed."

That jolted another memory that really resonated. I remembered a quote that had been attributed to Princess Diana's sister in the weeks leading up to the royal wedding. Apparently Princess Diana was having serious reservations about her pending marriage to Prince Charles (and we all know how that turned out!) Great Britain was abuzz at this fairy-tale-in-the-making and there were all manner of commemorative souvenirs for sale. When the former Diana Spencer told her sisters Sarah and Jane that she wanted to call off the wedding, one of them said, "Too late, Duch, (the family name for Diana), your face is already on the tea towels." Just like my big box of monogrammed towels. Too late, I thought . . . the towels are already monogramed.

Somehow I came to my senses. I decided then and there that I wasn't going to let a gift of monogrammed towels get in the way of my happiness. I wasn't about to marry a prince, and he certainly didn't treat me like his future queen. I didn't want to end up like poor Lady Diana. Just like that, I made up my mind that I was going to call off my wedding. And I felt better immediately.

I did keep the towels, though. They were fabulous. I also kept the bathrobe. In fact, I just threw the last of my monogrammed towels out about a year ago. They wore like iron and I used them every day. The only problem was I would occasionally have to explain to my guests why my towels had that unfamiliar monogram. I can't help it if I'm practical.

No. 3: Fear of not finding someone else to marry — this was the one and only chance

I wondered if anyone else would want to marry me . . . If there would ever be another person that I would want to marry.

I believed that he was the best I could get.

I thought he was so good looking. I never thought that I would get the chance to marry someone like him.

Many women were afraid to call off their wedding because they thought this was their only chance to marry. For whatever reason: they were getting older, they couldn't picture anyone else, or they were in a rut. They thought that they *had* to go through with this marriage, or they would end up alone.

What is ironic is that everyone we interviewed has gone on to a much happier life. Even more telling is that most of their lives have taken wonderful twists and turns beyond their imagining. As one woman who called it off told us:

I remember sitting all alone on the couch in his house wondering what I should do. I knew I had to call it off, but I was scared. I was 29 years old and couldn't imagine meeting another man. It's sad, but I didn't want to be alone. All of my friends were married. However, I was smart enough to know that I was bet-ter off alone than in an unhappy relationship. I didn't like my options — but I called it off. I am so glad I did!

One thing I always tell people who are in a rut, or depressed about their current life situation is that you never know where your life is headed next. I couldn't have dreamed up what happened to me in the years after I called off my wedding. I got a great job, found a great guy (I wasn't looking) and ended up get-ting married. We have three wonderful kids and I never looked back. I could barely see out of the hole I was in at the time — but I had enough faith in my-self to call it off.

Too many people get married because they have put blinders on — they only see what is right in front of them. They have limited their possibilities. Like the woman above, you must have faith in yourself! There is something better out there for you and it may or may not include getting married.

No. 4: Belief that the relationship would improve after the wedding

This is a biggie. Do not be tricked by this one. Marriage does not change a person. What they do now is what they will do later. In fact, any bad habits or behaviors will be magnified after marriage. If you have any doubts about this, please see Chapter 5, which explains in living color what happens when you marry the wrong person.

Even though the "bloom was off the rose" already, I thought that things would get better once we were married.

I didn't think that he would change — I just hoped that I could change enough to make <u>him</u> happy someday — that someday he would find me worthy of a compliment (or at least stop finding fault with me).

I desperately wanted to be married; I told myself he would be different after marriage.

I had the delusion that it would all work out . . . I guess I thought he would mellow out.

I was 26 years old and this was the time I always thought I'd get married and start to think about starting a family.

I have never figured out why I continued to stay with him. We were friends and enjoyed one another's company at times. Our sex was not enough for me; our relationship was not enough for me. I think it was the first time I decided to be in a committed relationship. I thought that we had to grow and change . . . that things would change after we were married. I still don't know.

I really wanted a family and I didn't realize at the time that you can't change someone. I really thought he would change.

I didn't walk away because I didn't have the emotional strength even when I knew down deep it was not right. I thought maybe I could change him into something I wanted him to be and live happily ever after.

No. 5: Time invested in the relationship

I was young, I wanted the dream wedding and we invested what I believed at the time to be sooooo many years into the relationship.

We had dated for several years. I didn't want to waste that. It was like it was too late to turn back the clock.

We had dated for a couple of years. Neither of us was getting any younger. I thought I better marry him so I didn't end up alone.

Far too many women end up wasting even more time with the wrong guy by falling prey to what we call the "wasted-time trap." A few years wasted in a bad relationship won't seem so long in the big picture of your life. What about the time wasted in a bad marriage? Stop the clock and get out now.

No. 6: Fear of publicly admitting a mistake; shame, embarrassment

I did not want to admit I had made a huge mistake the entire time and kept thinking I could make things work.

I did not want the embarrassment of calling off a planned wedding.

Two things stopped me from calling it off. The first was pride — I did not want to admit that my parents were right (they had never liked my fiance), and I did not want to admit I had made a mistake.

It's never pleasant to make a mistake — particularly a very public one. And there is no getting around the fact that if you call off your wedding, you will have to admit to everyone in your life you made a mistake. You'll have to tell your friends, neighbors, co-workers, and hairdresser (the list goes on). But think about this: Once you admit this, it is over and done with. You admit you made a mistake and that's that. It is out there in the open. Sure a few people might snicker behind your back. But your real friends and loving family members will support you. They will be proud of you for having the courage to call it off. One woman told us:

I told a lot of family and friends. It was the most embarrassing thing I ever had to do. I had already had a bridal shower with all of my mom's friends. I already had my dress. The thing that was a relief was that no one gave me any trouble about calling it off. Later, I became a little angry at family and friends for not saying something to me sooner!

And don't forget. If you get a divorce, you'll still have to do the EXACT SAME THING. You'll still have to admit you made a mistake. Save yourself the trouble. How's this for embarrassing?

He didn't show up at court for our divorce. His mother was a legal secretary so she replaced him. I had to tell the court (in front of the entire courtroom) that because he had been unfaithful to me, I had been given a venereal infection. I was very embarrassed but my wonderful sister-in-law (my brother's wife) gave me support at court.

Keep in mind that there may be a few folks who tell you that canceling your wedding is a big mistake. They may try to talk you out of it. But what do they know? The gut feelings belong to you — no one else.

You will be surprised how supportive everyone will be. Everyone we interviewed who called off their wedding received tremendous support. One woman said:

My parents told me they supported me 100 percent — and so did the rest of my family. Evidently, all my siblings and even my aunts, uncles and cousins who had met him had major concerns.

People who "always" make mistakes and people who "never" make mistakes

We had a big light bulb moment when we repeatedly heard statements like this:

I had observed my sister making many mistakes and getting in a lot of trouble. I didn't want to do anything wrong — I never did anything wrong. I felt I couldn't call it off — that would be the "wrong thing" to do.

There are some women who try to never make mistakes, and other women who feel they always make mistakes. They both gave the same reason for going ahead with their wedding. *They didn't want to make a mistake.* One woman said:

I had made a whole series of very public and painful mistakes in my early twenties. One of which was running away to the country, getting pregnant, and marrying a good-for-nothing guy. I had three kids with him and spent years getting my life on track. I was preparing to finally remarry — a really nice guy — but a guy I knew was wrong for me. As the day was getting closer, I wanted to cancel. But I just couldn't. I felt like I had made so many mistakes in the past, I didn't want to raise that whole issue again. I didn't want to risk making another public mistake. So I went through with it.

Everyone makes mistakes. It's okay to admit when you are wrong. Nobody's perfect — perfect people do not exist on this earth. There are only people who *think* they are perfect — and they are incredibly annoying. So admit your mistake. It's better to face up to a mistake beforehand instead of going through with one to save face.

No. 7: Financial concerns associated with canceling the wedding

There's no question that there are short-term costs associated with canceling your wedding. But remember, there are many more very nasty, unpleasant, and complicated long-term costs of *not* canceling your wedding. Whether you cancel your wedding six months, six days, or six hours before it starts, you are going to lose some money. Deposits on everything from the reception location, the band, the caterer, flowers, cake, etc. may be gone forever. Take the time to add it all up and see what it will really cost you so you will never second guess yourself. Determine exactly what the number will be. Let's look at a hypothetical wedding:

$1,500	deposit on reception location
$500	deposit for florist
$3,500	non-returnable wedding gown
$500	deposit to hold the date for the band
$1,250	spent on plane tickets for honeymoon
$8,250	

So the bad news is that this bride knows that she will lose $8,250 by canceling the wedding. That is the bottom-line number. Yikes, that sure seems like a lot of money, but think about the costs of splitting half of your assets, hiring a $250-an-hour divorce attorney, and being responsible for half of your ex-spouse's debts. As one woman told us:

I canceled my wedding six months to the day beforehand. I had not purchased my wedding dress yet, or thought out a lot of the details. In fact, that was one of my red flags . . . I kept putting off the wedding planning because I knew that I didn't want to go through with it. Fortunately, the only money I lost was the $1,500 deposit on the reception location. I consider it $1,500 well spent!

The good news is that if you get on the phone immediately, then clearly and rationally explain the situation to your wedding vendors, there is a chance that you can get some of your money back. If the reception site gets booked after you cancel, they may even consider refunding all of your money.

Another woman spent years paying off debt from her canceled wedding:

My parents told me they would help me with whatever financial implications there were [for calling it off]. It cost approximately $40,000 to break off the engagement. I felt strongly that since it would be my choice and not my fiancé's to break the engagement, I needed to pay for these expenses. (I was working at a non-profit at the time and not making much money so this was a huge step for me . . . it made me know I really wanted to do this. It took me five years to reimburse my parents.)

Even after all that, she was *still* glad she called it off.

This brave woman canceled her wedding when she realized her fiance was having doubts about their pending marriage: She shares her story:

After about three years of dating, I realized that he really just couldn't commit so I broke up with him. We went our separate ways for several months and then he wanted to get back together. He said he loved me and missed me and wanted to get married. He promised me he was 100 percent ready. I loved him and trusted him, but even as I accepted his proposal, somewhere deep down inside I had doubts. We planned a wedding for six months later. About two months before the wedding, I quit my job and moved across the country to be with him. I sold my furniture at a garage sale and basically got rid of everything I owned in preparation of our life together.

Soon after moving cross country, she realized that he was once again having doubts. (We will hear more from this wise almost-bride in Chapter Nine). She ultimately called off her wedding just two weeks before the big day. She tells us what happened:

The wedding was planned for only about 120 guests — not huge. After he called my family and my bridesmaids, my friends and family did a phone chain for my guests and my ex-fiance took care of calling all of his guests. He returned the gifts that had been sent to us with notes of apology. I was paralyzed, pretty much in "la-la land." Thankfully, my family took over.

My mom called all the venues to cancel and tried her best to negotiate the band, florist, and photographer out of their cancelation fees. We did lose all of the deposits. My fiance later reimbursed my parents for these expenses. My dad added up all the expenses that people were out. This included the deposits my parents had lost, bridesmaid dresses that had been purchased, my teacher's salary for six months, and the furniture that had been sold so cheaply at a garage sale. My dad prepared a letter requesting reimbursement [from my fiance]. I also kept the engagement ring (at my fiance's suggestion) that was worth roughly $10,000. I later sold it and used it as a down payment on my first house. I can't remember the total amount that he reimbursed, but I would guess that it was around $30,000.

At the time, some people remarked that it was incredible that he did all of that, because he didn't have to. But, what he did was what he should have done to clean up his mess. I believe it was absolutely fair and the right thing to do. The fact that my sister was involved in a serious relationship with his brother — and he didn't want to cause strife there — undoubtedly helped me garner that financial support from him. I don't know if he would have done what was fair and right if that had not been the case.

Fortunately, her fiance took full financial responsibility for the cancelation of their wedding.

No. 8: Confusion about canceling a party vs. canceling a relationship.

Can you tell the difference? The challenge is admitting that what you really want to cancel is the relationship itself. Unfortunately, people get so caught up in the details surrounding the ceremony and reception they feel they have to go through with it. They are paralyzed by the thought of telling their friends and family, the florist, and the caterer that the wedding is off. It seems silly when you look ahead. Will the caterer be there when your future husband is out drinking every night with his buddies? Will the florist help you out around the house when your husband refuses to do the laundry?

Many women knew they should cancel the relationship itself — but the party got in the way. If you think of it this way, it may help you see things more clearly. Ask yourself:

1. What is stopping me from calling off my wedding?
2. Is my hesitation related to any of the following issues?

• Money spent on dress, flowers, shoes, reception.
• A feeling that it is too late to cancel the big party — caught up in the momentum.
• Embarrassment over telling my wedding party that the party's off (quit picturing your friends in their taffeta bridesmaid dresses; they are your friends first).
• Disappointing people who are excited about "the wedding".

These are all issues related to canceling a party. Don't let the party planning issues "muddy the waters."

Next ask yourself:

1. **Deep down, do I really want to cancel the entire relationship?**
2. **If the answer is yes, make a list of all the reasons why you want to cancel the relationship.**

For example:

He is disrespectful to me. He has really treated me poorly through the wedding planning process and I know it will get worse after the wedding.

OR
I can really see some major family problems brewing. His mother does not like me and he does not support me. I have talked about it until I am blue in the face and he will not acknowledge my concerns.

OR

He has a hard time keeping a job and always seems to blame others for his misfortune.

OR

He has a problem abusing alcohol and he seems to be drinking more. He gets very defensive when I talk about it.

We don't mean to be redundant . . . but . . . if we've said it once, we've said it a hundred times ... PROBLEMS WILL NOT GET BETTER AFTER THE WEDDING. This woman cites practically every single one of the reasons listed above as to why she didn't call off her wedding. Wait until you see how her story ended:

As we moved ahead with our wedding plans, my fiance voiced some minor doubts about getting married. We talked about it and then we moved on. This just escalated as the wedding got closer. Little by little he shared some information about this female co-worker he had befriended and that was having mixed feelings about getting married to me because of his feelings for her. I was very confused and not sure what it all meant. He said he still wanted to be married to me and we continued to plan the wedding.

As the wedding got closer it was harder and harder to look beyond that. I had kept all of the above information about this other woman to myself for four months. I finally got the nerve to tell my family what was going on. I then learned some information about my fiance and his "friend" at work that might have alluded to them being more than friends. He denied any of this and said she was just a neutral friend he could talk to about all the stresses in his life. I was so blinded by my white dress, cake, invitations, limo, and marriage that I couldn't think straight. We went to counseling for a while and were encouraged to cancel the wedding. I didn't want to at all. I was devastated by the thought of not getting married and not marrying this man that I thought I was in love with.

We looked into what it would cost to cancel all the vendors and to possibly postpone the wedding but we were going to lose all the money we already put into the wedding and talked about it and decided not to cancel it. I logically <u>knew</u> that he would not change. I also knew deep down that marriage would not *improve the problems we had and in fact, it would only make them permanent. Unfortunately, my heart was telling me that marriage was the commitment that he needed. He promised me he was going to be the husband that I always wanted. At this time my family voiced some concern but overall they just wanted me to be happy and I said I was. At the time, I honestly thought I was . . . or at least on the surface I was..*

So she got married anyway. She tells us about her wedding day:

Honestly I was so happy when walking down the aisle. It was a dream come true. I was in my church where I grew up with all my family and closest friends around me. I was in a very beautiful dress and having the wedding I always wanted. I do remember feeling happy that my fiance showed up. I was a little nervous about this prior to the day.

Did she do the right thing? Here's what happened after the wedding:

During our engagement, my fiance would not let me put our engagement announcement in the newspaper. He told me that I could put our wedding announcement in after the wedding. So about one month after we were married, I put our wedding photo and announcement in the local paper. He came home from work one day and was very angry that I had done this because his co-workers had apparently seen it and asked him about it. That's when I found out that no one at his work knew he had gotten married! He had never even told them he was engaged!

Things just got worse after that and I kept catching him in lie after lie. We had planned to take our honeymoon four months after the wedding. We had our tickets purchased and were ready to go. About a week before our trip my now-husband got a text message that I read on his phone. It was at midnight from his "friend" from work. It read "I miss you; I wish we were sleeping together." I was obviously extremely furious and hurt. He denied doing anything with her and kept telling me that he did not understand why she would send that. When I wouldn't stop talking about it he then turned it around on me and blamed me for invading his privacy and looking at his phone. He then played the victim so that I would beg him for forgiveness. I was so torn about what to do. We had not even gone on our honeymoon and I didn't know what to believe. He wouldn't admit anything.

After we both calmed down he thought it would be a good idea to go on the trip to get away and just concentrate on our relationship. This was a huge mistake. He was very mean the entire week and didn't want to do anything with me. He told me on our honeymoon that he wanted a divorce and would go see a lawyer as soon as we got home. I was devastated. Marriage to me was <u>forever,</u> but the day after we got home from our honeymoon, I moved out. The marriage had lasted barely four months.

Would she have been better off canceling this wedding? She tells us why she *didn't* call it off:

Ever since I was a little girl I wanted to be married and be a mom. He was the first boyfriend that I ever had who told me he wanted to marry me. I clung to that during our six-year relationship. I was scared to start over and thought that marriage meant the same to him. I thought that his having a wife was the commitment he needed to be loyal to me.

What has she learned from this experience? More importantly, what does she want to tell other women who are trying to decide whether or not to call it off:

If you are having any doubts at all, do not do it. Life is too short to be unhappy. If it is meant to be, then it will happen. You must take a step back to figure out your thoughts. I would highly recommend pre-marital counseling. You must stick with it until you work through all of your issues to make sure you are doing the right thing. Often there are so many influences like family, friends, co-workers, the wedding plans, future life plans, etc. that it is hard to work through what YOU really want. Talking to a neutral party can really help you figure that out. Don't marry if you are not sure . . . it will just be harder later if you realize it after the wedding.

Calling off your wedding is not easy

We understand that it is a very difficult decision to make. But, once you know in your heart (and gut) that it is the right decision, the really hard part is acting on it and calling it off. Don't wait for an "obvious reason" or an "easy way out." Only you know the real reasons, and it's not likely that your fiance will make it easier on you or more understandable to other people. As two women told us:

Oh, I wish he would have cheated on me! It would have been easier to tell everyone that is why I called the wedding off — it was something that would have made sense to other people.

There was nothing dramatic to cite as a reason I wanted to leave, so I just went through with it. Once the wedding planning was underway, it was hard to say — "I am wrong about this relationship . . . we are just not compatible." I didn't want to admit I was making a mistake — I would have felt stupid. If I could have told everyone that I caught him in bed with another woman, everyone would have understood.

The things we do to avoid canceling a relationship!

In the spring of 2005, an Atlanta woman ran away from home four days before her big Southern wedding. Her disappearance led to a nationwide search and 24/7 media coverage. Three days after she disappeared, she called her fiance from Albuquerque, New Mexico. and told him (falsely) that she had been sexually assaulted by a man and a woman. She repeated these false claims to investigating officers, which resulted in a felony indictment. This could have cost her up to five years' imprisonment. She ultimately pled no contest to these charges and was sentenced to two years' probation and 120 hours of community service. She was also ordered to pay $2,250 in restitution for the cost of the local law enforcement's search. Upon her return, the runaway bride issued a statement that basically said she could not explain why she ran away and made up this outlandish story. Instead of calling off her wedding, she took off on a Greyhound bus, went cross-country, made up a story and had her friends, family and an entire town worried sick about her.

Of course this is an extreme example, and there may have been deeper emotional issues at work here, but it shows what a pressure cooker those days leading up to a wedding can be. It also illustrates how easily we can make bad choices when we try to avoid dealing with a difficult decision.

The solution is within you

No matter what the reason, it's never easy to call off a wedding. But don't make the same mistakes so many women in this book did. Carefully consider your concerns and ask yourself the tough questions.

Unfortunately, there is no one-size-fits-all strategy that will give you the courage to call off your wedding. Each woman's situation is unique and different. What we *can* tell you is that you already have the courage within you. It's there. Every woman within these pages had the courage, but not all of them could find it at the time.

Call upon the courageous part within you and trust that it will guide you to do whatever it is you need to do to walk away with your dignity and self-respect. When you do this, then you can set about the difficult tasks of admitting it to not only yourself, but to your circle of family and friends.

Think about calling it off

It is easy to get overwhelmed by the thought of this monumental task. There are too many people to tell, the showers have been scheduled, the flowers have been ordered, and the towels have already been monogrammed. Rather than getting lost in all of the party-planing details, try this:
Think about what it would be like to tell just one person about your doubts and fears about your pending marriage. Maybe that person is your mom or your best friend. How will she respond? How do you *want* her to respond? Why did you pick this particular person to tell? Is it because you know she

will support you unconditionally? The answers to these questions will give you a clue about what you really want to do and what you want to hear.

How do you think you'll feel after you tell that first person that you want to call off your wedding? Many women told us that they felt like a huge weight was lifted off their shoulders after they called off their wedding. Picture it in your own mind. Can you imagine a huge weight being lifted from your shoulders? Maybe you can visualize it as thousands of balloons being released to the sky. Whatever imagery it might be for you — a weight, a bunch of balloons, it is important to picture yourself taking that first step. You might actually be surprised by how liberating this decision will be.

Don't try and talk yourself out of what you are feeling. It is important to stop and pay attention. Don't dismiss any reservations you are feeling as "just jitters." You need to carefully examine what you are feeling, your fears and concerns. The next chapter can help you figure this out.

Ask a trusted friend to recommend a counselor or therapist. It's often easier to share your deepest fears or worrisome secrets with a compassionate, trained professional.

Remember, the long-term cost of a bad marriage far outweighs the short-term embarrassment or financial cost of a canceled wedding. Need proof? Go back and re-read Chapter 5 to remind yourself what you have to look forward to if you marry the wrong man. Don't say "I do" until you re-read them.

Chapter 8

JITTERS vs *Cold Feet*

Love and doubt have never been on speaking terms.
Kahlil Gibran

Playing alone in a bad neighborhood

In the course of researching this book, we went to several online wedding forums and message boards tagged with topics such as "cold feet," "jitters," or "second thoughts." Two things quickly became clear: First, there are a lot of people trying to figure out the difference between jitters and cold feet. They are desperate to figure out whether or not they should call off their wedding. Second, there is a lot of conflicting (and sometimes scary) advice out there.

While online forums can be helpful, they also can be akin to "playing alone in a bad neighborhood." The good news is that you are reaching out for help. You're taking the first step to address your concerns. But who are these people offering advice on whether or not you should marry? What are their qualifications? The value of personal advice from complete strangers can be questionable.

Another source of conflicting advice is the wealth of online articles available at the click of a mouse. If you do a quick Internet search on jitters or cold feet, you will find hundreds of articles on the subject. While some of the advice is right on target, other suggestions will leave a conflicted bride feeling even more confused. Written by well-meaning experts, the advice is often vague, with a "one-size-fits-all" approach. "Pre-wedding jitters are normal," they assure you. "Every bride or groom feels cold feet at some point." This may be true. Marriage is a huge transition. Change can be difficult. But there is a big difference between feeling nervous about the transition from single to married and having serious doubts about the relationship itself. And we believe that every woman knows deep down what she is feeling. Unfortunately, our overall impression is that most women are tempted to take this online advice, chalk up their feelings to jitters, and push aside their doubts. And as we have learned, when women ignore their intuition, they always regret it.

What are jitters and cold feet?

Cold feet is a slang term that means *fearfulness or timidity preventing the completion of a course of action.* [i] Jitters are defined as *nervousness; a feeling of fright or uneasiness.* [ii] By definition, cold feet is more specific as it relates to taking (or not taking) an action. Having the jitters means an overall sense of nervousness.

Most brides will tell you that they experience a bit of nervousness leading up to their wedding day:

• Will the florist show up on time?
• Will I stumble over my vows and embarrass myself?
• Will I cry?
• Will I faint at the altar?
• Will my little brother/aunt/uncle/cousin embarrass me at the wedding?
• Will the best man bring his new stripper girlfriend to the reception?
And so on . . .

All are common concerns before the big day. These are planning issues, temporary concerns that revolve around the actual event itself, not the relationship.

Change can be a source of jitters

Jitters also can stem from the tremendous change that is about to occur in your life. Going from single to married is a significant life change that should be met with some trepidation or fear. Just like the old adage says, "Living alone is like magic; all of your bad habits disappear." It's hard to give up your own space. As a single woman, you have the luxury of leaving your dirty clothes on the floor without being scolded. You only have to worry about feeding yourself. You can do whatever you want, whenever you want. You can hang a picture without having a two hour discussion about where to put it! Another way to better understand jitters is to look at other jitter-inducing events outside the context of marriage, events such as:

- A new job
- A completely different haircut
- College graduation
- A party where you don't know anyone
- A new puppy
- A start-up business

Just thinking about some of these things might make you nervous or fearful, but typically we face the fear and make a decision about whether or not we want to proceed. Without the issues of romance clouding our judgment, it's easier to make a decision — and sometimes that decision is a simple NO.

Cold Feet

Cold feet mean that you have doubts about a pending action or transaction. Brides aren't the only ones who experience cold feet. Investors get cold feet. Home and car buyers get them, too. Cold feet before the wedding means that you are having reservations about getting married. Unfortunately, it's a lot easier to be cool and analytical about buying a house or car. When love and loneliness get thrown in the mix, that's where the trouble begins. When your feet feel cold — no matter what the circumstances — you need to pay attention. Any of the following thoughts about your pending marriage should be cause for concern:

- I feel like I am settling for him.
- I don't like how he treats me.
- I hope our relationship will improve after the wedding.
- I don't think he is going to be a good husband.
- I have to go through with this because we have been dating for so long.
- If I don't marry him, I will never find anyone else.

These thoughts revolve around the *relationship*, not the wedding ceremony or reception. These are not temporary issues and they should not be ignored.

What's the verdict: cold feet or jitters?

So how do you know if what you have is just normal pre-wedding jitters or if that frozen feeling in your feet is really trying to get you to run in the other direction? **If you are feeling nervous or scared because you have questions about *the relationship itself*, then yes, you have cold feet.** Here's what our brave panel told us about how they distinguished between jitters and cold feet:

I knew it wasn't pre-wedding jitters when everything in my mind, heart, and soul screamed that I was doing the wrong thing. In my previous relationship, my son's father and I talked about getting married (before the pregnancy occurred). I was on cloud nine. On my end, everything felt right with him. Unfortunately he ended up feeling differently, so we never married. This time around, I was the one with the reservations. I think you just <u>know</u> when it is right and when it is wrong. You have to listen to your gut.

I just knew, deep down, that in the long term, it was not going to work. That's all.

I recently married the right man and I can tell you that this time I had no jitters on my wedding day. It was the happiest day of my life. When you are in a relationship with someone you are not truly happy with, it shows in every aspect of your life. When I called off my first wedding, I knew that I could not go through with something that I was not positive about. I could not lie to myself anymore and make it seem like I was happy in a relationship where I was really miserable.

I guess I knew that I wanted to call it off because I couldn't articulate what I really loved about him. It just became more and more clear that I was marrying him because of issues with myself and not because of our relationship.

It was so much more than jitters or cold feet. It was all wrong. I just knew that we were unsuited for one another in the long run. I was already unhappy with the relationship — and we weren't even married.

I knew it was more than jitters because I kept thinking. "How had I let it get this far — to the point of being married?" Why had I stayed in this relationship when I should have just gone out with him a few times and been done with it?

No jitters. Just deep down in my core <u>miserable</u> when I was with him.

By the time I called it off, I wasn't even thinking in terms of jitters or cold feet. When I confided in people, they tried to use these terms with me, to make me feel better. I knew it was more than jitters and it was something I could not brush off as "normal" or "typical". I knew the relationship was wrong and our marriage would not work. It was hard to face that.

Luckily we had not made any arrangements yet (because he was always too stressed out to talk about it), so there were no typical "pre-wedding jitters." However, I knew it was more than cold feet because after we decided to end our relationship, the first emotion I felt was relief. Of course I was sad, but more than anything I felt as if a weight had been lifted off my shoulders.

It was definitely not pre-wedding jitters. All of my reasons, and that feeling in my gut, were way bigger than nerves. This was the rest of my life we were talking about. I knew I didn't have commitment issues, just a hard time hurting someone who I purported to love so much. I really was more concerned with his feelings than with my own. I later learned that what I thought was love was really fear — fear of hurting him, fear of being alone, fear of what the future would hold for me without him.

Anne's story: My feet were ice cold and purple — and I still ignored them.

I was all alone in Chicago with my fiance. I didn't have any friends and I didn't have a job yet. I was in a state of limbo ignoring the warning bells ringing in my head. The only one who really acknowledged the tension was my cat, Ethel. She started spraying the walls around his dining room. She had never done this before. Disgusting, I know, but since she couldn't talk, she was trying to say: "Get out! What are you thinking? This is crazy!" My cat knew I was making a mistake and was telling me in her unique kitty way. I have no doubt that Ethel was responding to all of the stress and tension in the house. She knew I was unhappy.

As the days passed, it seemed like every time I turned around, I was smacked in the face with the mess I had gotten myself into. But for whatever reason I kept moving forward like some sort of passive robot. I was beyond questioning my cold feet or jitters. I knew we were completely incompatible. Our ideas about what marriage meant were so different. It was worse than that; neither of us had really formulated our own vision for what we believed marriage to be. I think we both thought that this was just the next step in our relationship. But I felt stuck. I was just trapped there and I had no one to talk to about what I was feeling.

I went to look at wedding gowns one day and tried one on. I was depressed, sad, and sick to my stomach. It was zero fun — a chore. I can still see my reflection in the mirror. I felt like I was dressed up in a Halloween costume. I was all alone. There were several other groups of people at the bridal shop who were looking at dresses. They were having a grand old time — laughing, crying and sharing a special moment. There were giddy bridesmaids, crying mothers, and joyful brides searching for that perfect dress.

And there I stood, all alone thinking, "Damn, not only do I not want to marry him, I don't even think I like him."

You are brave enough to face this!

When faced with a difficult decision, it's human nature to want to take the easy way out. If we are seeking advice on a problem, and we read several articles that assure us we are normal, it gives us permission to drop our concerns about the issue. That's why it's important to listen carefully to the one person who always knows what's right for you — and that's *you*. But how do you tackle such a difficult decision? Where do you begin?

Your inner voice

We all have conversations with ourselves. *"Those shoes are fabulous!"* **"But you can't afford them right now."** *"I know, but I should be getting that raise soon."* **"You really need to save your money**." The part that wants you to have those shoes is probably the same part that is critical about how you dress, how you look and feel about yourself, how much more successful you would look if you just had those shoes. Your true self, that little voice in your head, knows that money is tight right now and you already have two maxed-out credit cards. Which voice do you listen to?

The same kind of dialogue goes on within us when we are in a relationship. *"He's really attractive." **"But he's not very respectful to other people."*** *"He's just really confident." **"No, he's arrogant."*** *"Well, he has a really stressful job and does not always have time to be nice to people." **"He's not very respectful to you."*** *"But he says he loves me and maybe he will change."* When we don't listen to our inner voice, we almost always get into trouble. By the time most of us heed the warning, we feel stuck and we feel like it is too late to turn back. It is never too late!

You have a choice. What is your inner voice trying to warn you about? That voice inside of you — the core of who you are — is likely trying to tell you to call off the wedding. If anything in this book made you sit up and say, "That's exactly how I feel!" then there's your answer. The answers you seek can be found in someone else's mistake. The people we interviewed spoke very candidly about the intimate details of their relationships. They have the benefit of hindsight and were willing to take a closer look. They can tell you what they did wrong — it's their gift to you. They knew they should have called off the wedding, but something stopped them. What's stopping you?

How can I be sure?

So let's get back to the question we asked at the beginning of this chapter: is it cold feet or jitters? Take this quick multiple choice test and find out.

Q. You are feeling nervous about your wedding. Which of the following best describes the source of your concerns?

    A. Planning the wedding and reception
    B. Giving up my life as a single woman

C. Giving up my life as a single women and the stress of planning the wedding and reception
D. My relationship with my fiance
Your answer is:___?

If you answered A, B, or C—it's probably just jitters. If you answered D, you most likely have cold feet. Now consider the following:
Imagine your life with him five years from now. How do you *really* see yourself?
Do you see yourself living an authentic life or will you just be pretending?
Is he the wrong guy for you? Why or why not?

After working through these questions, how do you feel? Do you and your fiance have permanent or temporary issues that are troubling you? Are you simply nervous or do you have reservations that are preventing you from taking the next step … down the aisle? If you are still not sure, consider this:

If you could walk away right now and cancel the wedding, free of fear, free of guilt, free from embarrassment and financially free, would you do it?

Would you? Be honest. If you would, then this is not "normal, pre-wedding jitters." You've got cold feet.
The next chapter is filled with true stories from brides who canceled their weddings. They share their red flags, gut feelings and how they diagnosed their own cold feet. They also share what went down when they told their fiances it was over. None of them said it was easy — but none of them regretted it either. Read on to get the scoop.

---

[i] Cold feet. Dictionary.com. *The American Heritage® Dictionary of the English Language, Fourth Edition.* Houghton Mifflin Company, 2004. http://dictionary.reference.com/browse/Cold feet (accessed: July 27, 2008).

[ii] jitters. Dictionary.com. *Dictionary.com Unabridged (v 1.1).* Random House, Inc. http://dictionary.reference.com/browse/jitters (accessed: July 27, 2008).

Chapter 9

Calling it off: **TRUE STORIES**

When in doubt, don't.
Benjamin Franklin

A subject no one likes to talk about

Do you know how many weddings are canceled each year in the United States? Well . . . we don't either. We searched high and low to try and find that particular number, but it does not exist. We were just curious.

While we didn't find the number of canceled weddings, we did quickly find out that it is a subject no one likes to talk about. We called wedding planners, florists, caterers, and photographers to discuss their experiences. While they were very pleasant, the minute we raised the issue of canceled weddings, we often heard a sharp intake of breath or their voices dropped to a whisper. "Oh, yes, that does happen *sometimes*," they said, almost as if they didn't want to be associated with such unpleasantness. "It's fairly uncommon." Our personal favorite response was, "That doesn't really happen to us." Their attitude was that they were not the type of florist that would do business with someone who would cancel their wedding! When probed further, they admitted that it does happen, but apparently they were concerned that just talking about it might stir up some bad luck.

We spoke with one prominent catering executive whose company has a long history of handling the grandest events in his large midwestern city. Here is what he told us:

If you are talking about weddings that are canceled in the time frame of 7 to 14 days before the scheduled date, I would say that we have only experienced that about ten times over the last twenty years. However, if you are talking about weddings that are canceled further in advance, say three to four months, I would say that number is about 10 percent.

We asked him about the logistics of canceling:

We require a 50 percent, non-refundable deposit to reserve the date. So if you cancel after you have paid your deposit, we do not refund the money.

Usually it is the father of the bride who calls to cancel. Most of the time, people realize that it is cheaper to go forward and have a party anyway, since they have already spent the money. That seems to be the trend lately . . . they go ahead and celebrate, even though it is no longer a wedding reception.

With his many years' experience catering weddings, we asked whether it was obvious when a couple's wedding was a mistake:

Yes, absolutely. There is no doubt in my mind . . . it is written all over the face of the bride or groom. There is a difference between someone displaying the nerves associated with a big event vs. someone who is just going through the motions. All of our staff can recognize this at a wedding reception. We also see it in the temperament of the bride or groom leading up to the event; when they are unpleasant or difficult to deal with. It's as if they take their frustration about their relationship and upcoming wedding out on those who are serving them. An angry bride or groom is usually an unhappy bride or groom.

As we mentioned in the preface, it was much harder finding women willing to talk about their canceled wedding than it was finding those who knew their marriage was a mistake. The women who got married anyway were much more willing to air their dirty laundry about their mistaken marriage and subsequent divorce. And air it they did — cheating, lying, alcohol abuse, chronic unemployment, you name it. So why was it harder to talk about a canceled wedding than a miserable marriage and messy divorce? Our theory is this: The women who went through with a marriage know what a terrible, life-altering mistake they made because they lived it. They experienced the day-to-day misery of an unhappy marriage. They were willing to expose all the skeletons in their marital closet to prevent someone else from making the same mistake.

On the other hand, many of the women who found the courage to call off their wedding still don't completely understand how lucky they are. Perhaps the ladies who *did* talk to us understand that they dodged a bullet. What about those who did not want to talk about it? Maybe they were just private; or maybe they still don't recognize their own bravery and how much wisdom they have to offer.

We will never know for sure. We are grateful to everyone who even *considered* participating in our survey.

What's it like to call it off?

So let's hear from some women who *did* cancel their wedding. Let's see what it's like to call it off. Keep in mind: if the florist feels bad talking about it, how must the bride feel? Everyone who participated in our survey answered the same questions:

What were some of the red flags that concerned you about your fiance?
What was the "final straw" that led you to call off the wedding? Was there a specific event that triggered it?
What did that little voice inside of you have to say about it?
Would you describe it more as a little voice telling you something or was it more physical, e.g., headache, nausea, knot in stomach? Combination of voice and physical feelings?
Did you tell anyone else (besides your fiance) that you were calling it off? Did they try to talk you out of calling it off? Were they supportive? How did their support or lack of support make you feel?

Red flags spell trouble

Red flags are red flags. The red flags spotted by the women who called off their weddings were no different than those who did *not*. They ignored them, too. They looked the other way for a while. But eventually, they knew that the red flags spelled trouble and they had to pay attention. Note that these red flags are remarkably similar to those you read in Chapter 4, from women who eventually got divorced.

This woman grew weary of her fiance's money troubles
As our relationship continued, he began to have <u>numerous</u> money problems. He borrowed a lot of money from me without much explanation. He also had a very poor relationship with his ex-wife.

These women had plenty of red flags to choose from

There were many red flags — these are just a few off the top of my head: Disinterest in going places with me and my friends; not wanting to try new things with me; a very quick temper; not having <u>any</u> meaningful conversations (or any conversations that lasted over one minute!); frequently being so frustrated that phone conversations were ended by hanging up; not caring if I didn't see him; me secretly hoping that he would not come to the town where I was attending school to visit on the weekends so I could actually have fun with my friends; his constant reminder that I was doing <u>everything</u> wrong; yelling at me in front of family for insignificant things; not caring where we went on our honeymoon or where we lived; not telling me who his groomsmen were going to be, even after 9 months. He told me "you don't need to know." My fiance had all the red flags!

He smoked, drank, ran around, and came from a broken family. He also was getting into scrapes with the law, fights, etc.

He was physically and emotionally abusive to me. He would tell me I was fat, unattractive and needed to work out, etc.

The main red flag that really got me thinking about calling off my wedding was my ex-fiance's propensity towards violence. He never hit me or threatened me, but I had witnessed times where he, in my opinion, over-reacted to situations. One time he started beating in his bedroom closet door, denting it (it was metal) because Sears had turned him down for a credit card. It truly scared me how angry he became over something so small and unimportant. I felt like eventually, I might become the punching bag for his anger, and this was enough to make me think twice. He also was a big dreamer, very unrealistic in his expectations of his financial future. He was always looking to "get rich quick." He constantly told me how someday he was going to take care of me, but in the meantime, I was working as a model and footing the bills for the both of us. I feel like that is OK if you are really in it together for the long haul, but he was smoking pot (paid for by my money), taking karate (with my money), going to college (paid for by me), and he had no plans to use that degree because he was going to be an entrepreneur. It didn't all add up and I felt as if I was being used.

Judgment and an unwillingness to commit is a definite red flag

There were two key red flags that were important. The first was that he did not like or accept certain aspects of my past and his dissatisfaction kept creeping back into our relationship as an issue. For example, he did not like the fact that I was once a smoker. He also did not like that I had lived with a previous boyfriend. I can now recognize that he did not love me unconditionally. The other red flag was my repeated nagging awareness of his inability to commit.

A needy fiance will be a needy husband . . .

The red flag was that he loved me more than I loved him. He was very needy. He was very jealous and wanted to spend all his time with me. He was really good to me but he was so insecure. He didn't accept me for who I was — he didn't like the fact that I was so outgoing and he would initiate a big argument if he felt he wasn't getting enough attention from me. I just knew I was settling.

My fiance didn't have a life outside of me. He revolved <u>everything</u> around me. He didn't have many friends, and he would never make plans with those that he had. I guess you could say he didn't have his own life. I was his life.

. . . And a jealous fiance will be a jealous husband

My fiance had been cheated on by past girlfriends and so he was always questioning my actions. At that point in my life, I was working full-time and going to college in the evenings. I barely had time for myself. Living under a microscope is never fun and if you do not have trust in a relationship, it is bound for failure.

The way he treats his family often reveals how you will be treated

His relationship with his family was my biggest red flag. He was an only child and had been born later in life to his parents. He was self-centered. I knew that he wasn't always as kind or supportive of his parents as I was toward mine. One time we went shopping with his dad and mom. His father was in his late seventies at the time and was beginning to show real signs of dementia. He had worked for many years in the part of the city we were traveling to so my fiance had asked him a question about traffic patterns. His father remembered incorrectly and we wound up going across a bridge that made it inconvenient to turn around and get back to where we needed to be. It was an innocent mistake that cost us ten minutes at the most. My fiance went absolutely ballistic. He called his father all kinds of names. I watched this gentleman who adored his son shrink into oblivion in the front seat of the car and watched his mother who was in the back seat with me almost burst into tears. It took me by surprise and really shook me to my core. That entire outing (there were more little things that occurred throughout the afternoon and evening) actually pointed out in so many ways how incompatible we were — we had such different life experiences and values based on those experiences that I just didn't see how we were going to make things work.

She knew his mother would be a monster-in-law

He was an only child and his mother always made me feel like I was not good enough for her son. It is hard to be around someone who makes you feel that way. His mother and father divorced when he was young and his mother had hatred toward his father. After my fiance and I were engaged, she met a man and became engaged and it was almost like she was "keeping up with us." Her ring had to be bigger than mine, her house had to be newer than ours, etc. It was never like she could just be happy for my fiance and me; it was like she had to beat us at everything.

Contrary to popular opinion, a big house and a big diamond will not bring you love and happiness

I look back now and realize that I was blinded by material things. I had a beautiful diamond ring on my finger, we had a new house, and he had a great job. I knew I would never want for anything, he gave me any and everything I wanted but he did not give me the love and happiness that I needed.

She understood it was all about him

He was more interested in how I could fit into his life than in merging our two lives together. He was not that interested in spending time with my family and friends.

The straw that broke the camel's back

We asked everyone to look back and try to describe the event that triggered their decision to cancel the wedding. Some people could not pinpoint a specific event — they just knew that it wasn't right and they couldn't go through with it. But most people were able to recall in very clear detail the moment they knew they had to call it off. Here are their stories about the "final straw" that ended their relationship:

My fiance and I had bought a new home together and decided to live together for one year before our wedding. He made a good living, so we ended up purchasing a 3,300- square foot home. I thought I'd be happy no matter what. Who wouldn't be happy living in this beautiful new place with a guy who adored both my son and me? Wrong! Everything inside me screamed it was horribly wrong. I didn't love him — not the way a wife should love a husband. After the first week of living together I had what I describe as a nervous breakdown. Even though I was living in a large, beautiful home, I felt like I was caged in a tiny jail cell. I couldn't breathe. I couldn't eat. I couldn't sleep. I cried every day and screamed at everyone. I knew right then and there that I would not be able to stay with him a minute longer.

I was home for a six-week break from college and thought seeing him more would be good for our relationship and help us communicate better. Instead, I was more miserable the more I saw him. And the more I saw him, the more we fought and the more I got yelled at for reasons I didn't understand. The last day we were together, we went over to his brother and sister-in-law's house for lunch. I was really upset when he told his sister-in-law it was my fault that we didn't know where we were going to live or have a house yet (this was eight months before I graduated). I decided to go play Guitar Hero with my fiance's three-year-old nephew. Right after he made the comment about where we were going to live, he yelled at me in front of his whole family and grabbed the guitar out of my hands because I pushed the wrong button. It was just a video game and he totally overreacted. I was really upset.

From the day he proposed, I knew that this was a big risk and probably not going to be the right thing in the end. There were a couple of things that finally led me to say no. I broke the engagement four months before the big day, on Feb. 13th. I know everyone says I should have at least waited until I got my Valentine's Day gift (which it turns out did not exist so I didn't miss anything). On the previous New Year's Eve, after we had gotten home from a party and gone to bed, the phone rang at about 1:30 a.m. It was a woman who I suspected he had a fling with, wanting to wish him a happy new year. Needless to say, this caused quite a discussion. While he did reassure me based on the way he spoke to her and to me that night, it definitely started warning bells sounding in my head.

A few weeks later, we went to a dinner party at a friend's home. My fiance wanted to leave early, and I said I wanted to stay with our friends. He began to criticize me and make disparaging remarks about our relationship. I told him he could go and that I would get my own ride home. He left, and the two other couples (his cousin and one of his best friends) asked me if everything was OK and whether I was sure we should get married.

The final straw happened when a close friend of ours passed away. When it happened, he was not supportive of my feelings. In fact, he refused to talk about the situation. For a while I convinced myself that it was a part of his grieving process that caused him to be so cold, but I soon realized that his actions were impacting my own grieving in a way that wasn't healthy for me. This made me realize that his priorities were himself and his work — period.

It wasn't a specific event; it was more like five months of things that kept accumulating. For example, he asked me to sign a pre-nup. He also told me that he would want to send any kids we would have in the future to boarding school. I would never want to do that. We also had many conflicting religious views.

I called my wedding off approximately three weeks before the big day. I had gone out with the girls for my bachelorette party and by the time I came home, the sun was about to come up. Needless to say, I had entirely too much to drink and barely remembered my own name, let alone the events of the evening. As I came into the home we shared, my fiance began to question me about where I had been and who had I been sleeping with, so on and so forth. It seemed like a never-

ending cycle of being hounded about my actions. (This wasn't the first time. He was always questioning my whereabouts. I couldn't go anywhere without him thinking I was cheating on him). After finally a few hours of the interrogation, I went to sleep and woke up the next morning (which was Easter morning) and I called my mom and told her I would be coming home. My mom said, "Oh, for Easter dinner?" I said, "No, forever." I told her that I could not live my life this way. I could not imagine being hounded every day of my life and I could not live this way any longer. If it was this bad before we were married, imagine what it would be like in ten years.

My final straw wasn't really some big, momentous event. It evolved over a few months. The wedding was nearing and I left the country to do some modeling in Japan and make more money to pay for the big day. When I was finally out from under his thumb, I realized how much I had going for me and that I didn't need him to supply my self-esteem. I became more independent and began to see how he had been manipulating me into becoming a more submissive woman. He was controlling, and it took getting away from him to see it. The more times I talked about him, or wrote in my journal about us, the easier it was for me to see our relationship the way it really was. I felt stronger and more empowered to assert myself and I realized that I had been afraid of him for so many reasons. It may seem like I "chickened out" by calling off our wedding from the other side of the world, but it was the smartest thing I could have done. He was unable to coerce me or threaten me or try to convince me that I needed him to be loved or successful. I really felt strong, capable, and independent away from him. My instincts to call it off from afar proved to be right!

The final thing that happened was that I put the invitations in the mail. I had been anxious for a period of time, but found ways to push those feelings aside. When I dropped the invitations in the mailbox, I was hit with a huge sense of despair.

Listening to your gut

We asked people to describe their gut feelings about their pending marriage. What was that little voice inside of them trying to say? They told us:

Someone called my parents' house and said "Whatever you do, do not let your daughter marry him!" When that happened I knew that I had to call it off. My little voice said "Someone is looking out for you and it is not your fiance."

My voice inside my head kept telling me, "You know this is wrong. You are not marrying him because you love him and can't imagine your life without him. You are marrying him because you don't want to be alone anymore and you are tired of the dating scene." Also, I knew that part of what appealed to me was that my fiance was quite wealthy and we would lead a very nice life if we married. I knew that I had a lot of self-confidence issues and that I had chosen to be engaged from fear of loneliness. I had agreed to the engagement because I didn't love myself enough, not because I loved him so much. So my little voice was saying. "Don't use marriage to hide from what you know you need to work on about yourself."

It was a very exciting relationship because he lived in Los Angeles and I lived in Kansas City. He took me all over the world on exotic and amazing trips. I was so crazy about him and I was so focused on that at first. But after awhile, I realized that I yearned for simplicity, something that fit into my life more naturally.

I had a nightmare the first night we slept in our new house. I found myself searching for someone who represented true love. Realizing that I might never feel "true love" again scared the hell out of me. The little voice inside my head said that I needed to take some time to myself to sort things out. I asked my fiance the next day if he would give me some alone time in our house, that I really needed it to gather my thoughts. He left for a measly 45 minutes! When I asked him why he came home so soon, his response was, "Where am I supposed to go?" That was a <u>huge</u> sign to me that I would be <u>smothered</u> by this man the rest of my life. I literally couldn't breathe.

That little voice kept saying, "You can just get married; you can always get divorced later." At that time, I was working in a small law firm and became close friends with the attorney's wife. We talked a lot about how I did not feel 100 percent sure of my relationship and she told me that when she was younger, she, too, called off her first engagement. It helped to see someone have that much courage. She helped me realize that I did not <u>have </u>to get married; it was my personal choice.

I think I knew from the moment he proposed that it was wrong. I couldn't say no because he had proposed in such a public way that I didn't have the heart to humiliate him, so I said yes. Then once the "yes" was out of my mouth, I felt like there was no turning back. He was so happy, and I, on the other hand, didn't even want to call my parents! The deeper I got into the planning, the harder it was; the deposits were made, and the dress was purchased. I felt like I would be a fool if I called it off, but still, it just didn't feel right. I felt sick to my stomach more often than not. I had to battle with myself: which scenario was worse, going through with it or calling it off?

The voice inside my head told me, "He won't change. This is who he is; it's who he has always been. Staying with him will mean compromising what I need and deserve."

I had gone through every scenario in my head and I realized that I could not go through something that I was not 100% sure of. I did not want to put my family through the heartache of having a wedding and then it not working out. I knew when I did get married that I wanted it to be forever and I just did not see forever with him. (By the way, I just got married on October 25, 2008. I married my best friend and I couldn't be happier — I believe that everything happens for a reason.)

A voice or a feeling?

We asked them to describe their gut feelings. Did their inner wisdom have a voice? Or was it a physical sensation — a knot in the stomach? Butterflies? Headaches? They explained how they felt:

I definitely experienced more physical signs such as anxiety, panic, nausea, and deep depression. It's like these symptoms were under the surface while I was dating him and then when we moved in together, they exploded.

I would definitely describe my instinct as a sick feeling in the pit of my stomach, that sinking feeling you get when you know you have done something wrong. Like when you were a kid and you took something that didn't belong to you, you knew you were wrong, your gut told you so!

Honestly, I always had a gut feeling he wasn't the right one, even from our first date, but I went with it because he really pursued me. This was my first long term boyfriend and I thought that I just had to put up with things that he did. In fact, I tried to break up with him after 1 1/2 years because he cussed at me every day.

It was a nagging doubt all the time . . . I don't really remember having physical symptoms except when I actually did sit down and tell him it was over. Then, I did have a big pit in my stomach.

This voice physically manifested itself into sleepless nights. I would lie awake at night wondering what to do. Sometimes it was as if I could literally feel my heart breaking.

It was more physical — I wanted to throw up and then I felt fantastic once I called it off!

There was a little of both. I guess right before the bachelorette party, I began distancing myself from him. I was not as physically attracted to him and it felt like it took all of my effort to be happy with him. I did not want him to kiss me, touch me, or anything; it almost made me nauseous just to think about being intimate.

Leading up to the day we went to see the counselor, I repeatedly had terrible nightmares, in which I was in a natural disaster. Each night it was something different; an earthquake, a tidal wave, a fire, a tornado. No kidding; I probably had six nights of different nightmares, but I was always OK in the end. Somehow I would survive the disaster and then I would be sitting by myself in a peaceful mood. When I got back home, my therapist thought this was a very telling sign that I knew something was wrong and that I also knew that I would be OK in the end.

It was just a little voice. I never really felt any physical pain. Financial pain <u>yes</u>, physical, no.

Saying it out loud: I want to call it off

Admitting that your relationship is wrong is very difficult. Accepting it and acting on it is even harder. What role do other people play in this decision? Sharing deeply private information can be tricky because you never know how other people will respond. You also run the risk of them trying to talk you out of doing what you know is right. For the most part, everyone we interviewed said that telling others about their decision was difficult, but very cathartic. Their stories follow:

I told a lot of family and friends. It was the most embarrassing thing I ever had to do. I had already had a bridal shower with all of my mom's friends. I already had my dress. The thing that was a relief was that no one gave me any trouble about calling it off. Later, I became a little angry at family and friends for not saying something to me sooner!

I think my mom always knew that I was not truly happy with my fiance. It is that whole "mother's intuition." I think I was in that stage in my life where I just wanted to get married. My family was very supportive. Of course, my parents lost some money on deposits that they were not too thrilled about but they would have rather me called it off than to have been divorced a year later.

They were supportive, but it didn't really matter, because I prayed a lot beforehand and met with the priest to discuss it with him. I was very confident and clear-headed about my decision.

I told my boss. I had decided that I would break off the engagement and also move back to my hometown. He and I were talking about plans for the following year and so I felt I should warn him that I anticipated being gone within three months. He did not discourage me from breaking off my engagement but did discourage me from leaving my job.

I told my parents and friends. Everyone was extremely supportive and relieved. It was as if everyone knew I was unhappy before I did. In the end, all they wanted for me was to be happy.

I was working in Japan and living with a roommate who didn't speak English very well. Funny as it seems, I talked to her about my concerns and reservations. But the truth was, I was really talking to myself! It helps to get your thoughts out, and hear yourself tell the stories and the way you feel out loud. My roommate, of course, agreed with me. I don't think she really knew what I was talking about. Once I made the call to him, I felt like a million pounds had been lifted from my shoulders! I called my parents and they were thrilled; to say the least, they never liked him and I'm sure in the back of my mind I had known all along that they were right. That was definitely a boon to my confidence. It helps when your family agrees with your decision wholeheartedly, but I also knew myself that I had made the right decision.

My parents and best friend knew I was calling it off before my fiance did. My parents could see how upset I had been, so they were 100 percent supportive. Even though they loved my fiance very much, they knew I had to break it off. My friends felt all along that I was making a mistake when I got engaged. I've always been a hopeless romantic. I loved being in love.

I called off the wedding exactly one month and one day before the date. I felt so strongly about calling it off that I don't think I was weighing the consequences — it just didn't matter at all to me what people thought. In fact, I remember thinking after I did it that people might think I was a wimp or childish or afraid of moving (because I was going to move far away from home, to Dallas), but to my surprise, all these random girls (friends of friends of friends) called me to congratulate me on being so brave. It was so nice.

Anne's story: Guess what? — It's a boy!
That's great — I want to call off my wedding.

We were in the middle of a heat wave. As an unemployed gal, I was free to sit by the subdivision pool and read. Although I was looking for a job, I had a lot of unstructured time. (Oh, who am I kidding? Yes, I was looking for a job, but I was kind of half-hearted about it. Deep down I really didn't want to commit to a job in his hometown because I was feeling so conflicted about our relationship and marriage.) So yes — I was reading a lot of books at the pool. I would stake out a lounge chair in the back corner and watch all of the neighborhood moms and kids do their summertime thing. It was here where I began to think ahead to what my married life — right in this very neighborhood — was going to look like. And I didn't like what I saw in my mind's eye.

First of all, my fiance didn't like to spend time outside, and I did. I Loved the heat. Loved the sun. Loved swimming. There was a clubhouse and pavilion adjacent to the pool with a playground and barbecue pits. The neighbors gathered here all summer long. I knew my fiance wouldn't stick his big toe in the water and there would be no barbecuing for us. He wasn't much for socializing, either. I tried to imagine what kind of a dad he would be as I watched the kiddos splash in the water. It was sort of grim. We really hadn't even talked about our plans for a family. I had always hoped that I would have children. But when I thought about it, I couldn't see myself having children with him. In fact, the thought of being tied to him for life through a child was a very unpleasant one. And yes, I was still engaged to him! What sort of logic was that? Looking back it is really hard to believe that that woman by the pool was me! None of it makes any sense. Why would you be engaged to a person who, when pressed, you can't imagine having children with? This is how confused I was.

It was at this point that I successfully completed the required fourth and final step to marry the wrong guy. I had 1) stayed in the relationship for the wrong reason; 2) agreed to marry for the wrong reason; 3) ignored the red flags; and 4) ignored my gut feelings. But somehow, my inner voice would not be silenced! I just knew I could not marry him and had to call it off.

What was my first step? The day after my pool-side revelation, my dear friend Kathleen called from a hospital in Dallas. Just one hour postpartum, she was bursting with the good news of her bouncing baby boy. And what did I say in response to her glad tidings? "I can't marry him," I whispered. "I'm going to leave him." In two brief sentences I managed to suck all the joy out of her announcement and drag her into my messy life. That's what friends are for! God love her — she instantly shifted gears and put on her friend-counselor hat. I can't remember exactly what she said to me but the bottom line was that she supported me. She told me that I should do what I had to do. She told me exactly what I needed to hear. Her support set the wheels in motion for my departure. I don't know if I ever properly thanked her for that. In fact, I don't think I even sent a baby gift. But hey — I was too busy returning my wedding gifts.

So 17 years later — here's to Kathleen! Thanks for being such a good friend. Your support and friendship helped me hear my inner voice and find the courage to take action. Oh, and congratulations on your baby boy! Didn't he just get his driver's license?

The secret is to do something!

We believe that there are more people who go through with a mistaken marriage than those who call it off. Do we have the statistics to prove it? Not necessarily — but take a look at the divorce rate in the United States each year. As you have just read, it is a difficult process to determine that you need to call off your wedding or end your relationship. Taking action on this knowledge is even harder. The women in this chapter displayed remarkable courage and wisdom by calling off their wedding. We believe everyone has the ability to hear their inner voice and act on their feelings — but something stops them. How can you tap into the courage?

Talk to a friend or relative. Don't be afraid to admit to others that you are struggling with your decision to get married. You don't necessarily have to rent a billboard in Times Square to share your feelings, but you know who is safe to confide in. You might even be surprised to learn about their experiences in relationships or discover that they have been in the very same place.

Read. We have included a resource section in the back of this book listing the books we enjoyed reading while researching this project. There are many books on this list that cover the subject of gut feelings and intuition.

Talk to a religious adviser or spiritual director. If you are involved in your church, synagogue, etc., seek out direction from someone you trust. They most likely have been trained to deal with situations like yours, and if you can approach them without shame or guilt, they could be very helpful.

Take the first step

Another approach is to take just a few small steps in the right direction. It's often overwhelming to think about everything at once. Take out that trusty piece of paper and make a simple to-do list. For example:

1. Call (name of friend) to find a counselor
2. Call counselor
3. Set up appointment

And then stop there!
Or . . .
1. Write down your reservations
2. Call (name of friend or trusted adviser) and make a lunch date
3. Review the list with them

Then stop there. Give yourself a little time to digest all of it before you decide the next three steps. Taking just a few steps forward may be all it takes to put you on the right path to self-discovery. You don't have to call off the wedding this very minute. You don't need to dump your boyfriend right now. You simply need to start the process of uncovering the fears, concerns, or stressors related to your current relationship or pending marriage. Once you do this, you may discover how courageous you can be!

Mothers often talk about how they would jump in front of a moving train to save their child. We need to be willing to do the same thing for ourselves. Protecting yourself starts by taking the first step in the right direction — and that means stepping *away* from that fast-moving marriage train.

A few words about therapy

We found it very curious that among *all* the women we talked to, just one woman said that she turned to a therapist to help her sort out her reservations about her pending marriage.

Soon after moving in with him I began to have this gnawing feeling that something was wrong. I just didn't feel like he was in a joyful, happy place and I sensed fear and anxiety from him. I suggested that we go see a therapist and talk about what was going on. It was during the counseling session when I realized for certain that this man did not want to marry me. It was only two weeks away from the wedding and I was completely devastated. I knew that calling off the wedding was the only thing to do.

The therapist was extremely instrumental in helping both of us. She helped him find the courage to be completely honest with me and tell me that he really didn't want to marry me, and she helped me come to the conclusion that calling off the wedding was the only choice.

She also told him he needed to do whatever I asked of him in regard to calling off the wedding and getting my life back together. I placed a lot of blame on him. From the beginning, I was very clear that I was not going to force him to marry me. I wanted him to be 100 percent sure. He told me he was certain and then I started planning everything; a wedding, a cross-country move, and a job change. This was all based on the belief that he was ready to marry me.

Even though some of the other women we interviewed worked with a therapist at some point in their journey, this woman was the only one who deliberately sought out a therapist to find the answers to what was troubling her. Why did she turn to a therapist? Was it because she was living far from home — away from family and friends? She explains:

First of all, I have a master's degree in counseling, so I am a big believer in the benefits of counseling. Even if I was still living in my hometown I would have sought the help of a counselor. A really good counselor is a caring, knowledgeable person who is not in any way attached to the situation and who can ask all the right questions.

We asked her how she summarized her concerns to the therapist:

It was so long ago that I can't really remember every last detail. I can tell you that I am a "say it like it is" type of person, though, so I can't imagine there was a lot of beating around the bush! I do remember feeling scared about what I would find out. I think deep down, I knew what the outcome was going to be.
The therapist was very skilled. She spoke to the two of us together first. Then, she asked me to leave the room and she spoke to him by himself. Then she spoke to us together, where she asked him to explain to me what he had shared with her. It was then that I learned that he didn't want to get married. She then talked to me alone about what I wanted from him in order to get my life back and made some suggestions to me. After that, she spoke to the two of us together again where I then shared with him what I needed from him. She asked him if these were reasonable requests and he of course agreed to do whatever it would take.

Sometimes people think that therapy "takes too long," or you have to "go back to the day you were born" to uncover the underlying issues. That's simply false. We asked this almost-bride to tell us how easily she and her fiance moved from the explanation of the problem to the resolution:

The therapist knew the gist of the problem before we even walked in the door. I had spoken with her on the phone that morning, and she met with us later that day. I think the whole session was less than two hours. The way she expedited my personal emergency was superb.

She tells us how long it took from start to finish:

We only went to the therapist together once. The decision was made to call off the wedding and I flew home within days. I moved in with my mom and went to therapy on my own for probably five or six sessions. This therapist helped me work through my grief and helped me focus on moving forward. I got very lucky and found a job within a couple of months of returning home. I was really fortunate because I am in education, and it is difficult to find a position in the middle of an academic school year. So anything is possible. Because I was able to secure a job, and with the money I had from the engagement ring, I moved out of my mom's house and bought my first house shortly thereafter.

Her final thoughts for other women facing the same situation:

I would highly recommend that anyone who is having doubts about getting married go and see a good therapist. If you think your fiance is the one having doubts about getting married, then I recommend that you go together. The key here is to get a really good counselor. Ask someone you know who is in the field, or ask someone you know who has actually seen a good one themselves.

Jen's advice:
Common obstacles to therapy and how to find a qualified therapist

It can be difficult to seek out a therapist and ask for help. There also seems to be a certain amount of shame and/or fear surrounding therapy. But as you can see in the above situation, the counselor was instrumental in helping this couple decide to call off their wedding. Let's look at the most common myths vs. facts regarding therapy:

MYTH: Therapy is too expensive.
**FACT: A good therapist today will typically charge $100
and up depending on what part of the country you live in.**

This charge is hourly; the typical therapy session lasts 50 minutes. However, do you really want to balk at this cost? As you have read, you cannot put a price tag on your happiness. If you spend just four or five sessions determining what you need to do regarding your relationship, life, and happiness, that will be money well spent! Need convincing? Go back to Chapter 6 and read about divorce.

MYTH: Only the real "crazies" go into therapy and I know I am not crazy.
FACT: Your mental well-being should be of the utmost importance to you.

Therapists do not work with just the severely mentally ill. In fact, many therapists agree that it's the healthiest, most balanced people that seek help for problems that are impacting their daily life. If depression and anxiety are interfering with your sleeping and eating, it's important to get some help. Talking to therapist can help you find solutions and get your life back in balance.

MYTH: A total stranger will not be able to help me with my personal problems.
FACT: One of the greatest benefits to therapy is having a trained, professional "outsider" help you see the situation without bias and prejudice.

A good therapist (and yes, there *are* bad ones out there), will serve as a guide to help you navigate the rough and heavy terrain of your life and your relationship. They will be there to help point out the pitfalls, hidden hazards, and road bumps that are hindering you from making the necessary changes in your life. A therapist can not *make* you change; however, he or she can offer a safe place for you discover what you need to do. A word of caution: if a therapist does claim to be able to *make* you change, it is time to find a different therapist. The bottom line is that therapy can be one of the most incredibly rewarding experiences you can ever have.

MYTH: I don't need to deal with any of this. I can ignore it and it will just go away.
FACT: Despite what you might be telling yourself, avoiding what is happening in your life will not make it disappear.

Sure, you can lock it all up and shove it in the back of the attic, but eventually something or someone will trigger you and it will come flooding back to you. Sort through it now.

If you decide to take a leap of faith and see a therapist, here are two important things to consider.

How do you find a good, qualified counselor?

Do your homework. Conduct some research. Check with your insurance company. They most likely will have a list of mental health providers that are in your network. It is a daunting task to try and pick someone from a list of hundreds. If you must use a therapist from this list, know that you will need to spend some time making the right choice. Talk to your primary care physician, your friends, etc., and find out if they can recommend someone on the list. Also, be aware that your insurance company will determine how many sessions they allow you to have and it is often less than what you will actually need. Then call each of the recommended therapists and try to get a sense of who they are over the phone. This is another example of trusting your gut! Not all therapists have a Ph.D. in psychology; it simply means that they have a doctorate in their field of study. If you prefer to see a therapist with a Ph.D., that is a good place to start. Other credentials to be aware of are LCSW (Licensed Clinical Social Worker), LPC (Licensed Professional Counselor), LMFT (Licensed Marriage and Family Therapist). The exact titles vary by state, and regardless of the initials behind their name, the key ingredient is that they be licensed. Every state has specific licensing guidelines that must be met every year. Most licensed professionals have at least a master's degree. It is *not* recommended that you see someone who claims to be a therapist but is not licensed to practice clinically.

Life coaching is also a new trend in the field of psychotherapy. If you choose to go this route, find out if they are licensed as well. Some therapists who are already licensed in their study are now calling themselves coaches.

Will my insurance pay for therapy?

Health care benefits are not what they used to be. Most insurance companies do offer some benefits for mental health, but they vary. If you have an HMO, you will only have access to the list of providers they give you. If you choose to go out of this network, you will have to cover the cost of therapy. If you have a PPO, you will have the choice of using a provider in or out of the network. If you use a therapist out of network, more of the cost will fall to you. Be proactive and find out what the specifics of your coverage are so that you are not surprised with a large invoice. You should also be aware that the insurance companies have access to your records, so if your privacy is something that you want to maintain, you might want to consider paying out of pocket for your sessions.

For specific information, please refer to the resources found at the end of this book.

In the next chapter, we will hear the words of wisdom from those who *did not* call off their wedding. If you are grappling with a difficult decision about your relationship or pending marriage, their stories are just what you need.

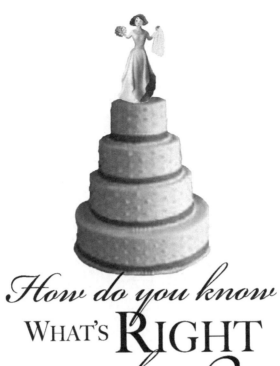

How do you know
WHAT'S RIGHT
for
YOU ?

Chapter 10

*Words of wisdom from women who ignored
their gut and got married*

*You did the best that you knew how. Now that you know
better, you'll do better.*

Maya Angelou

When in doubt, don't!

The women we interviewed for this book agreed to share their stories for one simple reason: They wanted to prevent someone from making the same mistake they did. Everyone we spoke to was willing to dredge up painful memories to stop *you* from marrying the wrong person. Listen to the caring words from a woman who wished she had called off her wedding:

Those of us who have been there before are standing around you, one arm linked around the waist of the person next to us and the other reaching out to you, to protect you and give you strength through these hard times.

When the student is ready, the teacher will appear

Experience is an excellent teacher — but you will benefit only if you pay attention to and learn from your mistakes. We spoke to dozens of "teachers" who were "experts" in the subject of ill-fated marriages. We asked them to share the lessons they learned from going through with a mistaken marriage. We have assumed that if you are reading this book, you are having reservations about your own relationship, engagement, or pending marriage. You are searching for answers about your conflicted feelings and concerns. As the old saying goes — *when the student is ready, the teacher will appear.* Here is the collected wisdom of our many "teachers." Are you ready to learn from their mistakes?

We posed the following question: **What words of wisdom would you offer to a woman who is currently engaged and having second thoughts?**

Listen to your gut instincts. Where does <u>your</u> true happiness lie? Pay attention to those red flags. Remember, when you're in the bottom of the barrel, you can't see the top. Cut your losses, move on, and don't throw good years away. I had feelings of unworthiness and worthlessness. My poor self-esteem got me into trouble, into the mess I found myself in. If I had been more secure, I would have never gone through with the wedding. You must be able to support yourself and live on your own. Do not be afraid to do this!

Never use marriage as a crutch for your issues, family problems, tragedies or even pregnancy. If you are having second thoughts, listen to your intuition. Talk to family members and friends who can see the relationship from the outside. They may have a better perspective.

It is a very valuable experience to live on your own. But even if you are living alone, you must be happy <u>with</u> yourself and <u>by</u> yourself. It is so important to be comfortable being alone. And that means not scheduling every minute of your time, always on the phone, running from one activity to another. You need to be able to sit at home on a Saturday night, all by yourself, and read a book.

Don't get caught in the trap of "When I marry him, I'll change him." And don't think that fatherhood will change him for the better, because it won't. If you suspect he won't be a very good father, you are probably right. Do not marry him because he will not change.

Do I wish I could do it all over again differently? Sure. I wish I would have waited for true love like I have now. My (current) husband is my best friend, lover, partner, confidant and father to my children. My ex-husband married the 15-year-old baby-sitter and had two kids with her. He is almost 50 years old and is still an asshole to me, his children and now his new wife. If your gut says run — you must run! No matter what, you must listen to your gut. It knows you better than you know yourself. It's your internal warning siren!

I finally came to understand that marriage is "who you are and who he is, coming together." Of course, you both must be two whole people coming together, but *the equation should be 1 + 1 = 3. Together, you are both better. So you must ask yourself: is it a good thing, a <u>better</u> thing when the two of you come together? My aunt was married to a real jerk. He never worked and she had to work like crazy to support their life. Their utilities kept getting shut off and I did not want to end up like my aunt. I just knew that I would have to support us because he had a hard time keeping a job and he was kind of lazy. Can you picture yourself in a bad situation with your fiance? If so, get out! Life is too short for that crap!*

Is the other person invested in this relationship? If not, take back control of your life. Move away from this person who is not invested in you — take a stand! Put your stake in the ground announcing "I am worth it!"

I should have waited until I was older to marry. I know that this advice is not true for everyone. There are plenty of people who get married when they are young and are happily married for fifty years. However, I do think that in this day and age, it is important to wait till you are older, having worked and lived alone before you marry. I guess it really boils down to being sure that you are making solid decisions in all areas of your life. If you are not making solid decisions, WAIT!

I lost myself in the process. I take the blame for not asking for what I wanted from my fiance and forcing him to propose to me. I forced the marriage. He didn't really want to get married. Later I realized that I had a marriage, but not a husband. It was doomed to fail!

It is important to pay attention to his family and how they relate to one another. I didn't do this and I should have. His and his family's behavior offered very specific clues as to who they were and what they valued. They were not necessarily bad people, just very different from my family. Little things become big things the longer you are together. I should have paid closer attention to what made him tick, money, success etc.

Don't try and script out your life because you may miss out on someone great.

My advice would come long before being engaged. Be sure you are comfortable and happy with just yourself. Without that you can never be happy with someone else. How you achieve that is well beyond my expertise. I would also advise someone to seek a partner whom you respect. You should think he is better than the best and he should think the same of you. A good foundation with similar values and beliefs definitely helps.

Listen to your instincts. Don't feel you have to get married to adhere to some timetable you thought up when you were an adolescent. If something doesn't feel right, address it with your fiance. Better to be an ex-fiance than an ex-wife.

Step back and take a good look at what you are about to do. Examine your motives for getting married. Talk to your partner and possibly try counseling. If he won't do that, then just end the relationship right then. Marriage is a lifetime commitment, not just a moment in time.

If the person truly loves you, they will be patient and want to work through whatever is making you have these second thoughts. DO NOT marry anyone you are not 100 percent sure is the person you want to spend your life with.

If you ever have thoughts that you don't want to do this, don't ignore them. It may not mean anything more than being nervous about making the right decision; that's normal. But don't ignore it. Talk to him about it, talk to your friends about it. Make sure you are still comfortable with making that decision.

Disagreements will happen, but disagreements are settled by conversation, not by yelling, name calling, telling the other person you don't know if you love them anymore. If you ever think or say you don't love the person anymore, then you don't. When you love someone genuinely, you love them even if you are not happy with them at the time.

It is much better to be alone and happy than married and unhappy. Trust me.

College is such a lack of preparation for the real world. Don't get married right out of college. Give yourself the gift of time. Hold down a job. Learn more about the real world. Getting married is what many women do to avoid facing the real world. If I had taken my time, and not rushed marriage, a lot more about his character traits and personality would have been obvious to me. Time would have revealed this. I really wanted a family and I didn't realize that you can't change someone. I really thought he would change.

If you have even an ounce of second thought, you need to figure out why. Do this even if it means calling off the wedding or postponing it. I've been married twice (the second time very happily). The second time there were absolutely NO second thoughts. My biggest worry was if the pastor was going to be there on time. I know without a doubt this was the man I was spending the rest of my life with. I couldn't say that the first time.

Now — take out that fluorescent highlighter and get to work!

Take a minute to reflect on what you have just read. This is the collective wisdom of many women who married the wrong guy. They have been there and done that — and they want to spare you the trouble. If you are seeking answers, this is the place to find solid advice. Before you read further, take out your hot pink fluorescent highlighter and start underlining the passages that stood out or resonated with you. Then reread those passages and ask yourself the following:

Is there a common thread among the passages I have highlighted? For example, are all my highlighted passages related to gut feelings?
Briefly write down these common themes in your own words; for example:
Fear of being alone
    Or
Marrying because everyone else is getting married
    Or
I think he will change

Sit with this information for a little bit — an hour, a day, a few days, whatever you need — then come back and reread the preceding words of wisdom. Write down on a piece of paper whatever comes to your mind. Let it flow — your fears, your concerns, and your reservations about your relationship. Don't worry about punctuation or grammar. This isn't a term paper. Let your inner voice guide your hand. Channel all of those pent up emotions onto a nice, clean sheet of paper. When you are done, the solution to your problem will most likely be spelled out in your own handwriting. Don't ignore it.

One final teacher: a woman who has had almost thirty years to reflect on her mistaken marriage speaks to you like a good friend.

Please understand that there are always other options. Yes, you might be hurting someone or closing some doors, but realize that hurting <u>yourself</u> instead is rarely the right answer in life. People who truly love you wouldn't want you to be hurt at their expense. People who don't love in the ways that you need to be loved definitely aren't worth the sacrifice! Listen to your heart. If it's uncertain and confused and even a little scared, then just announce (DO NOT ASK) that you're taking some time out to think through things. You're sorry for the pain and stress that this might cause others, (with wedding plans, money, reservations, etc), but you are taking care of yourself for once instead of others. Those who love you will understand. Those who don't...that's their problem, not yours. And if they react that way, then you have further reinforcement for not being a part of their lives. The guilt trips that people can lay on you are incredibly hard to take sometimes. Be strong. Decisions like this are very difficult and rarely clear-cut. Listen to your heart. Your caring side, the side that has been socialized since birth to take care of others at your expense, will be telling you that maybe it won't be so bad, maybe he'll change, maybe once you get away from here, maybe, maybe, maybe you could learn to tolerate X, Y, or Z. The tiny little voice in your head, that is learning to speak, only learns through situations like this. It's not very strong yet, but it's telling you that you're disappointing the main stakeholder — which is you. You're selling out your need to be loved in the ways you need to be loved (some of which you won't even know about until they happen) in order to make someone else happy and yourself only partly happy. Please don't do it. Your ability to be a happy, creative member of society and make this world a better place depends on *it. Take care of yourself. You are a precious gift to the world and your ability to explore those gifts to their fullest depends on you taking care of Number One: YOU!*

And finally, words of wisdom and advice from the clergy

What words of wisdom do the clergy have to offer us? Many marriages are officiated by a priest or pastor. Not only do they preside over the wedding ceremony itself, but they are often involved with some sort of marriage preparation. The Roman Catholic faith requires all engaged couples to participate in a course of marriage preparation. Other faiths offer similar courses or require that the couple meet privately with their pastor or officiant several times prior to the wedding. We discussed misguided marriages with a Catholic priest and Presbyterian pastor, and we found that their insights and observations were — well — surprisingly similar. Notice that both of them feel very strongly about the benefits of marriage preparation. They believe that couples who approach marriage with a *shared* commitment to success have a better chance of a happy, fulfilling relationship. Here are a few excerpts from those interviews, in their own words.

Marriage insights from Father Jim:

Catholics preparing for marriage usually complete a FOCCUS (Facilitating Open Couple Communication Understanding and Study) questionnaire. People always refer to the FOCCUS as a test. It is actually not a test — it is a tool for generating discussion. It is a good tool and useful "instrument." However, it can only identify potential conflicts; it doesn't solve them. One of the most important questions on the FOCCUS instrument is "I value keeping peace at any price." No one should agree with this. Because if you do, you are agreeing to live with something you can't bear, just to avoid a fight. Unfortunately, our culture often encourages us to say *anything* to get past an unpleasant situation in which you find yourself. The best-case scenario with marriage preparation is that a couple discovers issues they have not resolved — and then deals with them.

My dominant impression of engaged couples is that *people have no idea what they are getting into!* Sharing lives, sharing intimacy — it is harder work than a person could imagine. American society does not prepare us to get married as well as it should. Not as many people grow up in a household with both a father and mother these days — this does not allow for role modeling. People must understand that being raised in a solid, loving family shows a person how marriage is done. But if you do not have this role model, it doesn't mean you are doomed for failure; you must simply be aware of this missing insight.

I believe that the idea that marriage is about sharing and sacrifice has fallen out of favor. It is important to have a shared commitment to the institution of marriage. Love is a decision. You must begin every day by deciding again, "I am going to love you."

Do not get married if you have doubts. If you are uncertain, you need to work it out. Don't get married just because you have the reception hall rented. This is not a good enough reason to spend your life in misery. You may be able to resolve the doubts you are having; however, do it *before* the wedding because it may not be possible *after*. I tell couples that they must be mature enough to make the decision to marry. They must have the maturity and commitment to back up their decision. It's also important to be truly good friends — not just hormones that like each other. Are you comfortable just "hanging out" with each other? The bottom line is that your marriage has potential to make you both miserable, so it's not something to jump into if you have any doubts.

Marriage insights from Pastor Joe:

I am always glad when couples are interested in really working through things and talking about their relationship. Why? — Because 75 percent of the engaged couples are not interested in pre-marital counseling. They are more concerned with wedding plans, caterers, colors, and flowers. They are not engaged in the counseling, and their hearts are not in it. In order for counseling to be effective, they have to be receptive or it simply does not work. They are usually just going through the motions; they want to get it checked off the list. Something that strikes me, as a "man of the cloth" so to speak, is that people usually try to reserve the reception site first, and then they reserve the church. It's kind of symbolic of their priorities.

I have the right to refuse to marry people, and I have done that twice in 35 years. The first time, the groom showed up drunk. I did not marry them and had the full support of every single guest. The couple married later, but the marriage did not last long. The other time it was due to abuse. I knew that the bride lived in an abusive home and was trying to escape this — but she was about to marry an abusive person. I witnessed verbal abuse and saw signs of physical abuse on her. They got married anyway; unfortunately, I do not know what happened to her.

Some of the happiest people I know, people with wonderful marriages, don't have a lot of material wealth. They don't need it. Their solid, healthy marriage brings them all the joy and happiness they need. There are other people I know who have lots of material things, but no joy. It is an interesting lesson.

When we want to learn how to do something new, we seek out training and guidance. For example, if someone wants to become a real estate agent, they attend classes and take a test in order to obtain their license. It's a requirement for the job. They may also seek out a mentor in the field; someone who can show them how to navigate all the potential problems and issues that can arise when selling property. The more prepared they are, the better their chances of a successful real estate career. Men and women should approach marriage preparation with the same desire to succeed. Brides-and-grooms-to-be should be willing do the necessary work to prepare for a successful marriage.

I believe that when people are more intentional and see a counselor before marriage, they have a better chance of finding that biblical sense of "shalom"— peace —in their marriage. With preparation, they will find a true sense of contentment, happiness, and serenity when the two become one.

Learning from others' mistakes

The women who shared their stories in this chapter have been there, done that—and they wish they hadn't. They're hoping to prevent you from making the same mistakes they did. Did their advice make sense to you? Will you pay attention? Does it resonate? How will you respond?

Chapter 11

*Words of wisdom from women who listened to
their gut and called it off*

The only real valuable thing is intuition.
Albert Einstein

The few, the proud, the ones who called it off!

It's time to hear from the few, the proud, the ones who called it off. They paid attention to those gut feelings we've been talking about. They also found the courage to take action: they called off their wedding. How did they do it? What can we learn from them?

On courage

There is so much pressure on the bride-to-be — it's hard to stop that wedding train once it's barrelling down the tracks. We asked our brave panel why they think they had the courage to act:

I was able to do it because I had a lot of family and friends who supported my decision from the very moment I decided to call it off. Even the lady at the bridal store told me not to worry or be embarrassed; she said that I was not the first bride to return a dress! She then told me to remember to come back to her when I met my real "Prince." Three years later I did, and I went back to the same bridal shop and bought my dress!

I believe that part of the reason I was able to act on my instincts to call it off was because I spent time away from him, on my own. Reflecting, journaling, making new friends, having fun, and feeling like I was OK on my own was so important. I was out from under his choke hold and it felt good. I think taking some time and space for me was the key to tapping into my inner courage.

I think a lot of women (or men even) are scared to be alone. Society says that we need to find a mate, have a family, and grow old with someone. I was accustomed to living alone. I lived alone for five years before I moved in with my fiance. I never felt the need to have a mate, but at the time I wanted to have more children. So I guess I didn't let the fear of being alone stop me from doing what was best for me, and that was calling it off. In hindsight, I realize I do have every-thing I want: my independence. So many people dive into marriage when they know it's not right because they don't want to be alone; look at today's high di-vorce rate. Being single is NOT bad, and it's NOT scary.

Prayer gave me the courage! God helped me out of that mess — there's no way I could have done it on my own.

I think my courage came from the strong sense that this decision was bigger than me —the sense that, in some ways, I really didn't have a choice. I felt so deeply that it would be a disaster to follow through with it.

I knew I was lying to myself, trying to make myself believe that things would change. Ultimately, I had to do what was best for me and I had to make sure I was 100 percent happy before I could be happy with someone else. I knew that he was not the person that I could be truly happy with.

I think my courage came from understanding and knowing who "I" was sepa-rate of who "we" were. It took me a long time to find that, but once I did, I re-discovered what I deserve in a relationship. Also, knowing that my family and friends wanted me to be happy — over anything else — was a huge help for me.

Prayer for our relationship started close to day one, but intense crying prayers the last couple of weeks we were together let me know that the big guy upstairs had a better man planned out for me.

To be honest, I don't know. Nothing in my personal life up until that point would have said that I would be brave enough to do this. I have always had a lot of pro-fessional confidence but almost zero social confidence. I knew that I undersold myself, so to speak, in relationships and allowed myself to be taken advantage of but I just didn't believe I deserved more. Then, somehow I did believe it. I guess I'd have to say I finally opened my heart and head enough for God to plant warn-ing bells the size of Big Ben in there so that I would step back and say no. I will say that this was very difficult. All of my friends were his friends with very few exceptions. None of my close friends from high school or college had even met my fiance so I really didn't have anyone to bounce my concerns off of. It was a solo decision — one that made me realize a lot about myself. Some of my realizations were pretty; some were pretty ugly.

On regrets

The fear of making a mistake can paralyze us. We don't act because we don't want to do the wrong thing, or regret our choices. This fear often leads to bigger mistakes. As they say, the coverup is often worse than the crime. Failing to call off the wedding because you don't want to admit your mistake is a perfect example. Did our brave brides ever regret calling it off? Not one. But let them tell you in their own words:

Never. The year I called it off I often told people that I felt like I got an "A" on a life test. I was so proud of myself.

There was never a moment of regret. There were difficult moments. It was very difficult telling my parents, who really liked my fiance. It is wonderful now to be happily married with two kids. That, of course, further reinforces my perception that it was one of the best decisions I could have ever made.

NO! Not for a minute. (Although I wish I was still having a wedding!) As for the ex, well, he started calling and texting me things like "I see that you changed your Facebook status to not single" and "who is the new boyfriend?" and stuff like that. So I finally called him back after he left me several text messages. I told him that I think it would be best if we didn't talk to each other any more. And by the way, I took "single" off of my Facebook home page profile only because I felt that it was some kind of weird way to advertise myself. I don't currently have a boyfriend, but will be a very happy girl when I find a good one!

No. I never regretted calling it off. I do regret losing my ex-fiance as a friend. I tried to mend our friendship, but he wanted nothing to do with me.

I think that is one of the best decisions I have ever made in my life. I learned a lot from that day on and realized what kind of person I wanted to be married to. Everything happens for a reason and I think God has a plan for all of us. It may not be easy to see at the time, because I spent a lot of nights crying, but it all worked out and I married the man of my dreams.

No, I never regretted It — it was right from the beginning. I lived with him at the time. He had bought a lovely home for us to raise our future kids in. So, when I broke things off I had to find a place to live. When I told my fiance I wanted to call it off, he asked me to think about things for 24 hours and then we'd go to dinner and decide for sure. When I came home that evening to go to dinner, he was sound asleep on the sofa and said he didn't want to go out — I told him then that we were done. I called our friends and told them. They took me to lunch the next day and invited me and my two Rottweiler puppies to move in with them and their eight-month-old son. I knew then that this was absolutely the right thing for me to do.

I never regretted calling it off, even though he tried to keep me by warning me that I would regret it.

I only regret it when I let myself think, "Maybe he would have changed." However, when I remind myself that he didn't change after five years together, and how unhappy I was, the regret vanishes. I think it is more of wondering "what could have been" than regret.

This is a particularly disturbing story; in fact, we almost left it out. After some discussion, we decided it was important to show you what can happen in some extreme cases. The reality of a relationship with a mentally unbalanced person is that terrible things can happen. She called off the wedding — did she regret it?

I have never regretted it. Not for one second. The only thing I regret is that I stayed in the relationship so long. I like to think of myself as smarter than that. After I called it off, his daughter (age seven at the time and I think she was really the reason I wanted to marry him, because I was really in love with her and the idea of having a daughter), she cried a lot and wanted to know why I didn't want to be with THEM! I tried to explain that it had nothing to do with her and that she and I could still be friends.

Later, I realized that would not work. I had to change my phone number because he would call me at all hours of the day and try to get me back. Every time I changed my number the daughter would give him my new number, and tell him where I was going to be, etc. My ex-fiance called numerous times to tell me if I didn't take him back he would kill himself.

At first I tried to explain to him that it was not the end of the world. He finally called for about the hundredth time in the middle of the night and said he couldn't live without me and that he would kill himself if I didn't take him back. I COULDN'T TAKE IT ANY MORE! I said fine, just do it and stop bothering me. A week later I received a phone call at work from one of his friends telling me that he was found dead in his car. He had killed himself. I went to see a therapist (recommended by a friend). The therapist asked me why I was feeling guilty, and I realized I didn't really feel guilty; he was the one with the problems, not me.

What a terrible, traumatic event. It pains us to think about the little girl, too. Can you imagine what her married life would have been like? Her ex-fiance was clearly a deeply troubled man. She did the right thing by calling it off. And she was very wise to talk to a therapist and recognize that she was not responsible for his death. He took his own life. It wasn't her fault. How very sad.

On wisdom

If you want to know how to plant a beautiful garden, you talk to a horticulturist. If you need your haircut, you see a beautician. So who do you ask for advice about how to call off your wedding? Someone who has already done it. What words of wisdom do they offer you?

I would suggest that you find ways to know the difference between your inner wisdom and your fear, and to be able to trust and follow your inner wisdom.

People don't change, so if there is an issue you can't live with going into the marriage, it is not going to go away.

Think about the real reasons you are getting married. Is it because all your friends are getting married and you want to fit in? Are you afraid if you don't marry this guy you might not find anyone else? Do you think you need a husband for security? <u>Don't sell yourself short</u>. I didn't get married until I was 39 years old, and my husband was 44. Neither one of us had been married before! We have a beautiful daughter, a great life and a wonderful marriage. Good things do come to those who have the courage and wisdom to wait!

My advice to women who are trying to make this difficult decision is to take him out of the equation, in your mind, and figure out who you are. Then ask yourself: does he make you a better person? Does he allow you the freedom to be yourself and follow your heart? Is he accepting of who you are and where you come from? The truth is, you are marrying each other's families. No matter how far away you live from them, they are going to be a part of your relationship. Marriage is way bigger than a wedding and if you can't see past the wedding, at least postpone things. If he really loves you, he will wait until you feel comfortable. This time in your life shall pass!

Think about what it is you really want out of life. What will you be giving up by getting married to this person? What will you be gaining? DO NOT worry about how many people you will upset if you call the wedding off. It's your life and you have to live with your decision. Remember, being single has many awesome benefits. I'm living proof!

I rely on my religious faith. That's why I recommend that you pray very deeply for God to guide you, and pay attention to how you are feeling. When it's right, it is easy and natural, and now that I'm happily married, I am witness to that. It really was through constant prayer and focus on "marriage as a sacrament" that helped me see things progressively more clearly as "the day" approached, so that I could call it off with confidence and peace one month before. I put my trust in God, not worldly things, and it turned out so much better than I could have imagined.

I now work in a family law firm and it is heartbreaking to see the number of divorces. People marry for all the wrong reasons; they marry for money or stability, not for love and the bond of marriage. I can say if you are not 100 percent sure, don't do it. Marriage is not something to be taken lightly; marriage is a bond and vow that you make to another person, and if you don't feel you can uphold your end of that vow and bond then it is best to take a step back and view your relationship "from the outside looking in." I learned a lot from calling off my first engagement and God led me to my soul mate. It took me a few years but I found him and I am so happy to call him my husband.

What happened with me is not just because of my fiance. It takes two to make a relationship fully work and if you and your fiance are not both fully engaged in the relationship, then you should step back and take a deep look at things. If you have doubts and can't express those to your partner from the point of view of love and trust, then you have issues that should be dealt with before you go any further.

Don't get married just because you are afraid of what other people will think. You have to remember that what __you__ think is the most important factor in all of this. If you think "He'll change," he won't. If you think, "I'll change," you shouldn't have to! Also, if you have second thoughts, explore them; there might be something to those thoughts that are bigger than you could imagine.

Rely on those you trust, but also know that only you and your fiance really know what is and is not working in your relationship so only you can truly make this decision.

Pray hard. And know that this is someone you are supposed to trust and love the rest of your life. You should have a strong friendship with the person you marry.

If you find yourself saying, "It will be different when we get married" or, "It will be better," know the only way things change is if both of you want them to. So, if you __both__ aren't saying, "This is wrong for us and we are going to work on changing it," it won't change.

If any of your doubts about canceling revolve around what other people are going to think — just toss them! Because it doesn't matter what other people think. It only matters what you think. Are those other people going to live with you? No. Will they be there when you are sitting at your kitchen table crying because you are so unhappy? No, they will not. It all comes down to you. Will you be happy or not? That's all that matters — no one else's opinion matters. Don't let <u>anyone</u> talk you into a marriage that you don't feel is 100 percent right for you.

You can do it too!

So there you have it. These women demonstrated great courage. But they didn't have to jump out of an airplane or scale Mt. Everest. They simply responded to their inner wisdom and acted on it. And they had no regrets — not a single one. We never regret doing the right thing. Yes, it may be painful or embarrassing in the short term, but it's the right decision in the long term. Just ask the women from Chapter 10 who didn't call it off! They'll set you straight. In fact, they will do just about anything to keep you from following them down the aisle! Ask yourself:

- Do I have the courage to do the right thing? (Answer: YES. If your answer is no, re-read the section above on courage.)
- If I don't take action now, what will I regret? (Getting married to the wrong person? Staying in an unsatisfying relationship?)
- What words of wisdom do I need to hear right now? (What do I want to do? What do I really *need* to hear?)

If you are still undecided, the next chapter will share the words of wisdom from happily married couples. It may help you see your current relationship in a different light. Beware: the relationship spotlight can sometimes be very harsh.

Chapter 12

Listening to your gut: *Figuring out what you need and finding the courage to act*

A woman has got to love a bad man once or twice in her life,
to be thankful for a good one.
Marjorie Kinnan Rawlings

Gut Feelings: More than just intuition.

Are you thinking, "*Enough with the gut feelings stuff?*" Will you please just tell me what to do? Well, we can't. It's up to you to figure out what your gut is telling you. The good news is that the right answer *lies within you*. It's there — but you need to decide whether you are going to pay attention AND act on those feelings.

In his book *Gut Feelings*, author Gerd Gigerenzer shares the story of a friend who was in love with two women. The man couldn't decide which one he wanted to break up with, so he decided to turn to his gut feelings to uncover the answer. He tackled this dilemma by using an exercise oft-attributed to Benjamin Franklin. Apparently, Franklin's nephew was trying to choose between two different women as well. Franklin told his nephew to make a list of pros and cons about each young lady. Being the brilliant man that he was, Franklin had to go and get all mathematical about everything. He suggested that his nephew ascribe different weights or values to different character traits. For example, beauty might rate a little bit lower than intelligence. So his nephew made a list of weighted character traits for each woman and tallied up the score to arrive at his answer. Gigerenzer's friend tried the same approach, but when his answer pointed to Girl A instead of Girl B, his heart sank. And that's when he found the real answer. The facts and the numbers may have pointed to girl A, but his gut told him that it was Girl B who he really loved.

Try this yourself. But instead of choosing between two different men, you are really choosing between your current boyfriend or fiance vs. the single life (for now). Make two columns: one labeled **Together,** and the other **Apart**. Write all the reasons you want to remain in your relationship in the **Together** column. Think about his good qualities. Write down why he will be a good partner, husband, and father. Think about whether he brings out the best in you. Think about how he makes you feel, when you are together, as a couple. Then move to the **Apart** column and write down all of the reasons you would be better off breaking up. What are his bad qualities? What concerns do you have about his behavior or his character? What don't you like about him? Just let it flow. Walk away and come back to it if you have to. Then, once you have completed your list, take a look at the answers. Does your gut agree with the result of this exercise?

If you need more help deciding

We've talked about the four common mistakes women make that put them at risk of marrying the wrong guy. We told you about gut feelings and cold feet, doubt and reservations. We've defined settling. We've also told you about red flags, bad marriages and what divorce is really like. There is a lot for you to think about. But we've got one final trick up our sleeves. We are now going to share the collective wisdom of dozens and dozens of *happily married women*. Some have been married just five years and some for almost 50 years. We eliminated anyone who said she had the "perfect marriage." Why? Because there's no such thing as a perfect marriage and we doubted the wisdom of anyone who made this claim. Instead, we talked to women who identified themselves as "happily married." Sure, they have the same ups and downs, dry spells, and aggravation that we all do. But overall, they say they are very happy, content, and grateful for their husbands. It was fun to have a flood of *positive* surveys fill up our mailboxes. One woman said that she had initially hesitated to complete the survey because she had been aggravated with her husband for a few days. She called back when she was done and said it was just what she needed to do because it reminded her of all of his wonderful characteristics!

Look in the mirror

As we said at the end of the last chapter, sometimes you need to look at your relationship in a different light. You need to hold it up to a mirror to see what could be missing. These positive testimonies are that mirror.

There is no checklist that exists that will detail what you need for a happy marriage. Everyone has a different idea about what they want in a spouse. As one woman told us, ***"He is not a perfect man, but he is the perfect man for me."***

We each have different wants, needs, concerns, and desires. By reading the words of wisdom from a broad cross-section of happily married women, you may be able to uncover what is wrong or missing in your current relationship. But more importantly, it will help you articulate your vision for what you want and need in a future partner or husband.

We asked happily married women to share what they've learned about creating a fulfilling marriage. They share what they value most about their spouses, what they've learned, and offer words of wisdom for young women contemplating marriage.

The right guy: what's he like?

There are certain qualities that we all know are important in a spouse. Some of the bedrock characteristics include compassion, honesty, and respect. These are a given. But there are a lot of other qualities and traits that are necessary for a good, transformative marriage. Unfortunately, we don't always know what qualities we really want and need until we're trapped in a bad marriage or relationship. So let's hear it from happily married women. What are their spouses' best characteristics and how do they benefit their marriage?

My husband is quiet and is a very good listener. He is very helpful and tries very hard to please. He is fair with the children, both biological and step. He is a constant. Knowing that I have an attentive ear helps me to deal with problems that arise both at home and away from home. Being able to rely on my husband to help around the house — with the children and in other areas of our lives — enables me to get involved in things outside the home and have a well-rounded lifestyle. I can count on my husband in any situation, which is comforting and relaxing. All of these things help me be a good me. If I weren't a good me, I wouldn't make a good wife or mother.

My husband is intelligent, ambitious, kind, humorous, physically active, supportive, spiritual, and very forgiving. I share a love of nature and outdoor activities with him, and appreciate his knowledge about science and business. Humor has been our antidote for pain and anger.

My husband is gentle and patient. He is a good man with a lot of integrity and he works hard at being a good husband. He is not a perfect man, but he is the perfect man for me. His patience is required often in his relationship with me! He listens to me, tries to understand my moods, and sometimes just asks what he can do to help me. Other than my parents, I have never had someone love me as deeply as I know he does. Sure we argue, and we get on one another's nerves, but we always know it is temporary. Our relationship is built on the trust that we are both committed to one another. We have only been married five years, but I can honestly say that we have never had an argument so intense that I worried we wouldn't make it. Divorce or leaving one another is just not an option for us. We work at things until we resolve them. While that isn't always easy, our marriage is important enough for both of us to do so.

My husband is honest; I can always trust his words, never having to doubt or wonder. This provides security, which is a must in a strong relationship. He is also humorous. His ability to bring light-hearted fun and laughter to a situation makes life more bearable. And he is sensitive. Knowing he cares and is emotionally invested in our life together allows for intimacy.

He is <u>very</u> kind and forgiving, and thoroughly loves being a husband and father and grandpa.

He does not respond to events with anger, and never uses criticism or shame as a method of fighting. Yet he can hold his own and argue his position with kindness and is often more insightful and correct in his perspective. He is confident of his own views yet has the grace and stability to allow divergence and alternative points of view. He takes charge when he needs to and has the grace to use problem solving when I am out of sorts. He matches my moods and laughs often and well at the world's choices. He is also gorgeous at 70-plus and continues to explore new ideas with amazing enthusiasm.

My husband is honest, genuine, considerate, selfless, humble, and a great partner. These qualities benefit our marriage tremendously. In creating a good nurturing relationship these qualities are essential. I value the person he is, and try to be the best I can in return.

Committed — our family and our relationship comes first. He will speak up even to family when their actions or words interfere with how we believe. Thoughtful — he may not be a big romantic, but he knows when to surprise me with a clean bathroom or dinner for two — or when to give me space. Funny — oh so funny, with everyone in all situations. He may go over the line sometimes, but his humor solves more problems than it causes.

He is level-headed and logical whereas I am emotional. It balances out when we are making major decisions together. I appreciate that he is like that because it brings me back down to earth and defines things more clearly when I am stuck on the emotional side of a problem or decision.

My husband is very comfortable with who he is, and doesn't feel pressure to meet others' expectations. As someone who is always trying to please everyone, I found that refreshing! One of the first things that attracted me to him was his broad range of friends. He invited me to a backyard barbecue, and the group was comprised of an incredibly diverse mix of people (especially for Boston) from different races, backgrounds, creeds, careers, ages, nationalities, and abilities/disabilities. I had never been to a house gathering that was so interesting — and comfortable. "Who is this guy," I wondered, "who cultivates a wonderful group of friends like this?" He really sees the best in all people first, and considers everyone his friend — unless or until they prove otherwise. Just as he is who he is, he sees others for who they are — not what they do, who they know, etc. He's kind — particularly to those in need. He's very down to earth and practical — and yet has a very spiritual side. We share a sense of adventure, and of actively "building" a life, not just waiting for it to happen. He's goofy and funny in a way that totally cracks me up.

He is the kindest person I have ever known. I can count on him to be truthful with me and he listens. When we have hit some difficulty, those qualities shine through, so we can deal with the problem and not have do deal with his reaction to the problem before we can tackle the issue. He is really smart and sexy too. So it is hard to stay mad at him for very long.
Great sense of humor (always makes me laugh), very complimentary and kind, still says I am beautiful when I wake up in the morning and look like hell and

still says I am beautiful when I have gained 15 pounds. He is always very kind to me; every woman needs this! And every man needs this too; he is very hot and sexy to me and I let him know it!

He is the voice of reason. He rarely gets rattled about anything. While I am freaking out or overreacting, he always puts things into perspective.

He is a man of the highest integrity; he is as solid as a rock when it comes to life's issues. He has a good sense of humor and enjoys the simple things in life like being with the kids or working outside. I never have to worry about him or how he will weigh in on an issue. I can count on him, and he always sees things with great clarity. This helps us to work through issues without a lot of drama.

His priorities are in order — faith, family, and friends. He has a great sense of humor. He is intelligent, calm, and a good listener (which goes very well with a talker like me!).

He is very intelligent in his field and has multiple interests. He is a fabulous listener and communicator. We have many of the same interests, and he is always willing to try new adventures. We enjoy spending time together whether we are just "being" or actually participating in an activity. We do not argue very much at all, because he is always willing to talk about my concerns and feelings, and often agrees to disagree.

This woman speaks of her beloved, now-deceased husband. They were high school sweethearts and married for more than forty years. Their marriage serves as a model for all of their children:

He was an honest, polite, kind man with a terrific sense of humor, but above all else he never wavered in his love for me and his family. He always provided for us. He was by no means a saint, just a good man. I think his commitment to the success and safety of me and our kids gave our marriage a sense of peace, trust, and security.

This woman told us about her husband who is facing the challenges of a degenerative neuromuscular disease:

His best characteristics are his faithfulness and humbleness. He is faithful to his family and always makes sure that we are second in his life – right after God. He has such a humble nature – he never complains about his health or the unfairness of the cards he has been dealt. He has such a giving nature, but in a most quiet manner. He always does kind deeds without ever looking for acknowledgement.

Does a twenty-year-old woman want the same thing as a seventy-year-old woman?

We asked women to think back to when they were in their early twenties. We were curious about what they looked for in a date or boyfriend. What did their twenty-year old self think was important? What we were really trying to find out was whether or not the qualities they desired back then are still important to them now. They explain:

When I was younger and shallower, physical appearance was a big issue. If I were to find myself looking today — which I have no intention of doing — I would be more likely to look for someone who would be a good provider, someone mature, someone with strong moral values, a witty sense of humor, and intelligence.

This question made me realize how very much I have changed in 20 years! When I was 20, I wanted a good-looking, well-built guy who liked to go out and have fun and who had money to spend on me. Now, the qualities that I think are important in a good spouse are love, commitment, responsibility, friendship, shared dreams and values.

I wanted smart, funny, sensitive, and kind. I wanted to be very important to that person. Those qualities were important to me then and to me now.

Honesty was a really important characteristic, and so was overall goodness. I tended to date gregarious, life-of-the-party type guys that were arrogant. I married the complete opposite and I feel extremely grateful.

Then, I think having fun and finding someone "sexy" was major. I do think my husband of 28 years is sexy, but now a level head and "wisdom" are more important to me.

I think when I was younger, I had a "list" in my head of characteristics: ambitious, likes to do the things I do and makes me laugh. I didn't think as much about the qualities of the man as a person, but more about what he <u>did</u>, and how that related to me. Now, I think more about who he <u>is</u>, alone with me, and in the world. Qualities such as kindness and curiosity (about other people and the world) are important. Other important considerations include, loving to his family, conscientiousness, spirituality and humor. Yes, humor is still a key ingredient!

The qualities I looked for then are the same qualities now. Great sense of humor, kind, honest/ethical, God at the center of his heart, fun, someone who enjoys sports and staying active (and good looking). Most importantly, someone who likes to laugh! Someone who has many friends.

I think I often fell into relationships where I had to "fix" someone. After a few bad relationships I timed myself out and stopped worrying about being with someone. In the end what I needed was a man who was at least as strong as I am and who wasn't needy or undependable. Now the most important qualities are strength, humor and love. I married my husband without any expectations that he would change.

Looks were probably more important to me when I was younger than when I got older, though it wasn't critical even then. Kindness and compassion were always important to me. I was taught early on to look hard at the parents of anyone I dated — it would tell me a lot about that person. I noticed immediately how close his family was and what a good marriage his parents seemed to have, even though they certainly had their noisy Italian arguments. They reminded me of my parents.

When I was 20, I was dating a very attractive but boring man. I remember my friends asking me what I liked most about him and my only response was

always, "He's just so cute." I had no concept of what I wanted or needed in a re-
lationship and needless to say, we broke up. I constantly picked fights with this
guy, just to provoke emotion from him. I needed more than just good looks, and
even though I knew it, I refused to let go of him because he was CUTE! Being
cute is still an important quality, but I've learned that it really means nothing.
Looks fade, but a person who gets who I am and can hold up his end of a con-
versation and make me laugh — that is what really matters to me now.

While many women said they valued these key qualities in their twenties,
several admitted to seeking more superficial things, such as good looks or sexiness. No matter what your age, it's important to consider the traits you want
and need in your future spouse or boyfriend. It all goes back to being that
"calculating women" we talked about back in Chapter 1. What is your vision
for your married life? What do you need for a fulfilling relationship? Good
looks and sexiness are not enough. One woman sums it up best:

I needed competence and still do, I needed kindness and still do, I needed care-
taking and still do. The 20 and the 70 are not that far apart.

How have happy marriages influenced you?

Living in the reflected glow of a happy marriage can have a positive
influence on your own relationship. It's important to realize, however, that
your parents' happy marriage does not inoculate you from the possibility of
divorce. Likewise, children of divorce are not always doomed to unhappy
marriages of their own. What's *most* important is that you're *aware* of what
a happy marriage looks and feels like. Let's take a look at how the happy
marriages in these women's lives influenced their own:

My parents are happily married and have been for over 40 years. That is not to
say they have not had their share of ups and downs, but they have stuck by each
other even when one has let the other down. They have forgiven each other,
laughed at their differences, griped about them, too, but still manage to hold
each other's hand when walking together. This has made a huge impact in my
life and the marriage I now have.

Almost everyone I knew growing up had a happy marriage, or at least from what I observed. I grew up surrounded by good solid families that really showed me how important a strong foundation is. I valued how most of my friends grew up, and I wanted the same for our kids.

Many of our friends have happy marriages. It seems the key is respect for the other person, knowing that their weaknesses are probably your strengths and not something you have to change in him or him in you. We each have the missing pieces that the other one does not have.

The happy marriages I see are between people who have stable individual personalities. They share child rearing, chores, and other practical things as well as a similar "world-view." They also seem to share a willingness to change together.

My parents and grandparents enjoyed the other's company and made each other a priority. It has helped me look forward to my life with my husband, seeing couples who are successful with growing old together. It gives me hope. I have a friend who at 48 is now caring for her formerly athletic and active husband who is in a skilled nursing facility due to suffering a traumatic brain injury in a motor vehicle crash. It is hard, but the love is still observable between them. It has shown me that even in the worst of times, a strong and loving marriage makes anything tolerable.

I think my model for a happy marriage was my grandparents. They were married for 75 years! They were both strong and independent people who really cared for each other. They were funny together, and never really "lovey" or affectionate in front of us kids, but you could tell these two people would do anything for each other. They also totally put up with each other's quirks. I know they didn't have an easy life together, especially early on — several miscarriages and many disagreements. However, they were committed to many of the same things — a strong and healthy family above all. They also had their own interests. They died within 12 hours of each other, the day before Valentine's Day. The impact on me was that I understood and believed that a happy marriage could exist, but it wouldn't be idyllic! It also made me feel safe and comfortable and loved — and I came to recognize that feeling when I met "the one."

We have friends who got married at 18 due to a pregnancy and have been truly happy for 35 years. With everything pushing against them, they pulled together. They still play like a couple of kids. They respect and adore one another. There is nothing worse than a bad marriage, but a good one is one of life's great blessings. I have been married now for 24 years and wake up each day feeling loved.

The neighbors next door exemplify the love, courage, and faith it takes to have a truly great marriage. We have shared good times and bad times. They have taught me that in spite of great hardship, love and faith are always with us; they laugh even when they cry. I have come to realize that even when you think it is as bad as it could be, you can still love one another.

I was very blessed to witness my parents' marriage. They certainly lived through some really difficult times and I witnessed some of those. Yet they modeled for my siblings and me how to work things out, rely on their faith, etc. My dad always called my mom his "bride." It was clear that they loved each other. They were also quite affectionate — too much in my adolescent eyes sometimes.

My parents' marriage of 50 years has been a true inspiration to me. I have seen their love for one another blossom over the years, and it just keeps getting stronger. They have had a happy, faith-filled, loving relationship, and even though they have been through much sadness (the birth of their fourth daughter, who was di-agnosed with Down Syndrome, a precious angel lost at the tender age of 11 years, parent's and sibling deaths) they have never lost sight of the love they have for one another. My parents have always backed one another up when it came to raising their daughters, even if they didn't always agree with each other. They always kept a unified front, and my husband and I try to incorporate that gift into our marriage today.

My parents just celebrated their 40th anniversary. They truly love and support each other. I don't know what the next 40 years will hold, but it's my intention to do everything I can to get to my 40th anniversary with my husband.

Words of wisdom on choosing a spouse. . .

We've heard the words of wisdom from women who were married to the wrong guy. Now let's hear from some happily married women. What wise words do they offer on choosing the right guy? What's important? What should you think about?

Don't marry someone thinking you will change him. God created them as they are and you won't be able to undo him.
Romance, good looks, and sex will diminish over time. Make sure your relationship includes important factors like friendship, a shared interest in things, companionship, and genuine love for one another.

Before you slip the ring on your finger or say "I do," make sure to ask yourself these questions. Does he treat his Mom with respect? Does he treat his dog with respect? Does he actually listen to other people or just act like he does? Is he ethical in business? Is he spiritual? Can he balance his checkbook? Do you feel good about yourself when you are with him? Does he know how to make a bed? Does he really know who you are? If you answer no to any of these questions, run the other way!

Make sure you feel like you are yourself around him. Don't morph into something you are not because you will only regret it in the future. Try to find a balance between what he can offer you and how you can complement him. You can't put yourself first all the time, but you can't always put his needs first either. There needs to be a compromise at all times, and keeping track of who "won" last time won't get you anywhere. Make sure you love his not-so-great qualities too, because they don't go away!

Share common interests and values — friendship. And be able to laugh at yourself and each other. Be able to forgive yourself and your spouse.

Be open — your prince charming may not appear the way you have pictured him! Know yourself first, and then be curious about others. Don't expect that a spouse will fill all the gaps in your life, or be your perfect companion in every way

— *and don't let them make that mistake either. Pick someone who truly "gets" you, your strengths and weaknesses, respects and admires you, and vice versa! Be upfront in discussing issues like money, children, and in-laws, so you are both clear on what you'll tolerate and what you can't. Not everyone defines marriage the same way. Make sure you both understand you're on the same ground before making the commitment. Don't base your decision on looks, money, status, or anything else that can change – because it will — you need to make sure that if all those were gone, you would still want to be with him.*

I tell my children to start with happy. Choose someone who is naturally good-natured. You can't make someone happy so better to start with that. Be happy yourself. Choose generous. If a person can't part with money, they won't be generous in other areas either. Money is the easiest thing to give away so pay attention. Stingy shows up everywhere, in sharing yourself, in helping with the chores, in time with you and the children.

Make sure you are crazy about him and he is crazy about you. Make sure that you have the same goals. Talk about your goals, wants and dreams. Think about having children with this person and getting old with this person. Loving them forever. If that does not sound like something that makes you very happy, then you are not ready for marriage.

Make sure he is kind, treats you with respect, and is faithful and truthful to you. And make sure his love for you is as deeply rooted as your love is for him.

Choose someone who makes you laugh. Share some common interests. Know that what attracts you to that person will probably at some point irritate you. This is not a bad thing, though it is the very thing that creates a spiritual partner — someone who challenges you to grow and know yourself better.

The person you marry should be a match for you in the following ways: love, sex, money, and children. And he must match in all four. You can be sexually compatible with a person, but if he's broke and needs you to take care of him, say good-bye. It is so important that you hash all of these issues out <u>before</u> the wedding. Make sure you both agree on how to spend and save money. Make sure he *knows that you want to be a stay-at-home mom after the second kid. Make sure he loves you for who you are and exactly that. Make sure he knows what you like in and out of the bedroom and supports your ambitions. And you should be able to say the very same for yourself concerning him.*

Choose a man you respect, deeply love, and a man who wants to take care of you and your family. Don't marry someone who has an annoying habit you can't stand now, because it will only drive you crazy later. Marry the love of your life, a man you cannot live without, a man you would never want to let down, a man you want to love and cherish. Marry a man who already is a good friend to his friends and respects his mother. These are the characteristics of a good man who is marriage material.

. . . And words of wisdom on marriage

Finally our happily married women share their collective wisdom on marriage. What wise words do they offer a young woman about marriage? This book is filled with advice on how to marry the wrong guy. What do you need to know to marry the *right* guy? They share their insights:

Marriage is wonderful, difficult, all-consuming and can be completely satisfying. It is a work in progress every day! If you put as much work into the actual marriage that you do in the planning of the wedding, you will be OK.

Marriage is perhaps the most important decision in life. Know yourself well and know realistically what you need out of a relationship. Can this person meet your needs?

As wonderful as you may envision marriage to be, it is that much better. And as hard as you think marriage is going to be, it is that much harder. You don't make your marriage vows only on your wedding day; you spend each day of your marriage living out the "for better or for worse, or in richer and in poorer or in sickness and in health."

Bring your faith into your marriage, really listen to the vows you are taking at your wedding, and know that each day of marriage is a recommitment to those vows. Know that all the conflicts and hard times in your marriage are what make you fall deeper in love if you stick it out. The good times are precious but the hard times are what mold two hearts into one.

Plan on marriage being a life-time commitment. Make sure, as much as you can, that this is someone you want to live with for a long time, and be willing to grow old with him. Plan to not always get your way — figure that if you each give in on things that are really important to the other (presuming you can, in integrity), you can compromise on most issues that come up. Be willing to talk about things. Want to make the other person happy, but be sure you know how to be happy yourself. And know that there will be days/times when you won't be crazy about him; but know that, too, is part of the ebb and flow of relationships. Take time to enjoy yourselves as a couple, no matter how hard your jobs are or how many children you have.

Remind yourself it is forever. And anything that lasts forever must be well cared for. Listen to the logical side of your heart. When you sense huge red flags, know that they will not go away. Remind yourself every day you are a 50-percent share-holder in the company, which means that if you truly put your heart and soul into the relationship, there is a huge possibility that it will be successful.

Enter into marriage as a commitment rather than a trial, and know that marriage reflects the rest of life: it includes pain, struggle, and change. If there is no openness to change there can be no growth. Love changes faces — from early passion to a deep and abiding respect. You may not always feel like you are in love.

Marriage is at its core a partnership. It helps if you share some of the same values and goals. But it's also important for each partner to bring something special to the relationship — complementary skills, experiences, knowledge. If something drives you crazy about the person (he's a slob, she talks to much, whatever), it's only going to get more pronounced as you're together. Sometimes people can make small changes, but chances are, you're going to have to live with it! So choose before you make the commitment if this is something you can live with!

In the '70s when I was in high school, a teacher once gave me some advice, long before the phrase "What would Jesus do?" became popular. I was having a problem with a friend and he said, "Look at all the ways you can solve this. Then choose the most loving thing to do." Those words really stayed with me and I find that they work in our relationship as well. We don't keep score, we just respond with love and kindness. Laughter is essential. Whatever is horrible today won't be as big or scary tomorrow.

A healthy marriage takes work. Both people have to be willing to work at it, make changes, forgive, grow together, etc. Faith is a critical piece and a wonderful gift to a marriage. Look to healthy models of marriage as guides in how to overcome the tough times.

Be very sure that you want a marriage, not just a wedding. The wedding is one day; the marriage is your whole life. If you want a wedding, throw yourself a party and wear a white dress.

Marriage is an exciting, wonderfully frustrating learning experience. Be prepared to learn about yourself and the man you married and respond with laughter, loads of patience, some tears and frustration, but plenty of love. You will learn about the many depths of love and it will change your life forever. Tend to your heart and his, be patient, and give all that you can and more, and you will reap unbelievable love.

Jen's story: my happy marriage

Once I hit adolescence, I was pretty confident in what I wanted in a boyfriend. He would have to respect me, make me laugh, and above all, accept all of me, inside and out. There was also a big part of me that was looking for someone to rescue me and get me the hell out of my house. By the time I went off to college, it was pretty obvious that my parents were not happy and the thought of returning to that environment was depressing. I am not particularly proud of that part of me, but it was reality.

For me, watching my parents' relationship slowly deteriorate, in a sense, helped me to clearly define what I did not want in a relationship. Remember, "If you understand how to marry the wrong guy, you will understand how to marry the right one!" I was the poster child for this statement. I want to again reiterate that I felt loved by my parents. I just did not witness their love for one another very often.

I met my husband in high school and was immediately attracted to him, "metal mouth" and all. He was and continues to be a charmer! My dad used to call him "Eddie Haskell" (the insincere brown-noser from the show "Leave it to Beaver"). I never liked it when he called him that because it made him seem false; in reality he just did nice things for people. Back then I think my dad was skeptical of such behavior. When we first started dating, I was introduced to his enormous family. Many of his brothers and sisters had already gotten married and started having children. I had never seen a teenage boy hold a baby and actually enjoy it! I remember thinking what a great dad he would grow up to be and I was right. He held the door open for me, he liked my friends, he didn't judge my family, he never embarrassed me, he respected me, and he was a good person. It did not hurt that he was tall, dark, and handsome! Those qualities were and continue to be very attractive. Another important quality is his ability to forgive me and on the flip side, take responsibility for his own mistakes.

We dated for seven years before we got married. We were young and naive but we never doubted the decision we were making. And although my parents had a difficult relationship, his parents had a wonderful marriage. He brought that experience of living in a loving marriage to our relationship.

When we first got married, we were broke and lived in a teeny-tiny apartment. Despite the small size of our first home, for the first time in my life, I felt like I had some breathing room. Fourteen years later, we have survived the loss of his father, my parents' divorce, the purchase of our first house, health issues, job issues, the birth of our beautiful children, and financial stress. Yet through all of the joy and sadness, I have never once questioned his love for me and his faith in our relationship.

The one challenge we had then and continue to work on today is how we deal with conflict. He rarely watched his parents argue and my reaction when my parents were fighting was to run and hide. Needless to say, when a conflict erupts in our relationship today, I typically want to escape. You can imagine how well that goes over in our house! What he has shown me, however, is that no matter what, we will deal with our difficulties head on. He gives me time to retreat for a little while but then he gently wrangles me back in and we work it through, even if we agree to disagree. I never fear that he'll abandon me for having a different thought, opinion, or approach than he does. This is a complete 180-degree turn from what I observed in my parents' house. Conflict would flare up, tempers would soar, and resentments were bottled up until the cork eventually flew off that day in my parent's living room. I made a commitment to myself and to my husband to approach conflict differently, no matter how hard it might be. It is a commitment that we revisit often, sometimes even when we do it wrong.

I share my positive story with you not to make you feel bad about your own relationship, although I understand that might be a reaction. I share it with you so that you might start to tap into the part of you that wants a healthy marriage and to not just end up another divorce statistic. My life could have turned out very differently if my husband had not shown up or if I had not paid attention to him when he did enter into my life. There were plenty of wrong guys out there and they were seductive. In my gut, I knew better than to throw a good thing away. And although I would have gladly let him rescue me from my dreaded castle, he knew what I needed and has been right by my side while I learn how to "rescue" myself. For that I am grateful.

So how do you marry the right guy?

We've explained in great detail what you must do to marry the wrong guy. But we also promised that if you understand how to marry the wrong guy — you'll know how to marry the right one. Dozens of women have revisited their own painful past (and joyful present), in order to help you make the right decisions. We sincerely hope that you have taken their advice to heart and will apply it to your own life and relationships.

Have you gained an understanding of what you want and need in a partner? Have you defined a clearer vision of the life you want — and what kind of husband or partner you need to achieve this vision? Let's clarify something. Women don't *need* a man in order to be happy. But if marriage is part of your life plan, make sure you are not jumping into marriage for the wrong reasons, with the wrong man.

We want you to marry the right guy. The man who will add to your life, not subtract from it. We wish you much success in life and love.

Did you call it off? We want to hear from you!

As we said in the beginning of the book, we will consider the cancelation of any destined-for-disaster wedding a success story. The end of an engagement counts, too. We also hope that there are lots of bad boyfriends sent packing as a result of this book. If you call off your wedding or break up with your boyfriend after reading, please visit our website and tell us about it. <u>We'd love to hear your story.</u>

<u>www.coldfeetpress.com</u>

With your permission, we'll use your story on our website or blog to help other women find the courage they need to follow their gut feelings. Just like the stories in this book helped you — *your* story can help someone, too.

Thank you so much for reading our book. We hope that you found the answers that you have been looking for.

www.coldfeetpress.com

Love, Anne Milford and Jennifer Gauvain

Chapter 13

The man chapter

No man is worth your tears, but once you find one that is, he won't make you cry.
Author unknown

Technically speaking, there is no 13th chapter in this book

Did you ever notice that most high rise buildings or hotels don't have a 13th floor? Technically they do, they're just not labeled that way. It's all due to the superstitions surrounding the supposed unlucky number 13. Well, our book is like that, too. Technically we don't have a 13th chapter. We felt a little uncertain about inviting men into our book, but about a dozen men had responded to our survey, and we found the results interesting. So we're offering this bonus "13th chapter" that takes you inside the minds of *men* who went through with a wedding they knew was a mistake.

Overall, the women's reasons for staying in the relationship seemed to be slightly more complicated. That is, they often revolved around the fear of being alone, or the need to feel loved. On the other hand, *all* of the men we talked to failed to cancel the wedding *because they did not want to hurt their fiancée*. They often had other reasons, as well, but their first reason was that they did not want to hurt their bride's feelings.

Who's going to say "9 don't!"

Most of the relationships you read about in this book were extremely unhealthy. The women shared their stories of emotionally unavailable men. They told us how they had been lied to, cheated on, disrespected, or ignored. But we also heard from several women who were dating nice guys. The problem was, these nice guys were not the *right* guys. And as we've said over and over, if the relationship is wrong, the marriage will be wrong, too. And that's a no-win situation. So what's a girl to do? Who's going to be the one to shout "no, no, I really don't!"

Bad news ladies: it's your call

The most important lesson to learn here, no matter what the circumstances, more likely than not, *the woman is going to have to be the one to call it off.* Don't wait for your fiance to do it. If you know you are about to marry the wrong guy — *you* will need to call it off. It's that simple. Your relationship is not ideal, you may fight frequently, your communication may be poor, and you may struggle over many other issues with him, but he may be very reluctant to hurt your feelings by saying he doesn't want to marry you after all. So it's up to you.

Some men, like some women, stay in relationships against their better judgment and they get married even though they know it will be a mistake. The key difference that we found is that men felt a certain sense of obligation to go through with the wedding. They had to honor their commitment. Here, in their own words, are the reasons why they didn't call it off:

I thought that I had made my bed — now I have to lie in it.

I would have liked to have called off the wedding but I did not want to hurt her feelings — it was my job to make the best of it.

I was embarrassed to call it off and I didn't want to face everyone. I didn't want them thinking negatively of me. I put their feelings toward me ahead of my feelings about my life.

I recall thinking that I really didn't want to do this. But I felt like I had to because of all the promises made to her and to friends. In short, I felt trapped.

These men felt many of the same pressures to go through with the wedding. And they all lived to regret their decision to marry the wrong woman.

Final words of wisdom, this time from the men . . .

We gave the men the opportunity to offer advice to women who were about to make the same mistake they did. Here's what they chose to say: *My advice to those who experience similar situations is: listen to others, don't just take your own counsel. There is a lot of pressure on you — you are dealing with a commitment of a lifetime. You need to really work through this process, have patience and understand why you are getting married. Marriage is not an easy commitment and should not be discerned with the heart only.*

It is OK to be "selfish" and think of yourself when it comes to such a major commitment — marriage. You need to look at it from both sides. What is in it for you? What is in it for her (or him)? Are you better together or separately? I was taught that you don't hurt women, you honor your obligations etc. I was confused about what constituted being selfish vs. hurting her vs. what was good for me and for her in the long run. I had a strong sense of right and wrong. This caused me to go through with something that I shouldn't have. By going through with the marriage, it was more hurtful to both of us. I should have called it off.

Heed Barney Fife's advice: "Nip it in the bud." Do not go through with it, no matter what. The pain is not worth the brief embarrassment or any other problems you may encounter by calling off the ceremony. You'll be glad you did.

If you ever have those thoughts that you don't want to do this, don't ignore them. Talk to her about it, talk to your other friends about it. Make sure you are still comfortable with making that decision.

One man offered advice on choosing a spouse that sums it up best. We'll leave you on the "13th floor" with these final words of wisdom:

When it comes to choosing the right guy, you've got to trust your gut. All those other guys that just don't work out for one reason or another will help you weed out the bad guys. And that is how you will find the right guy.

We couldn't have said it better ourselves!

Anne's Acknowledgements

First of all, I must thank all of women whose interviews made this book possible. Without your stories, there would be no book. I know it was very difficult for many of you to revisit these painful memories. Your willingness to go "back there" and visit them anyway in the hope of helping other people was truly inspiring. Words can't express my gratitude.

I feel slightly guilty for not putting my dear husband Doug on the top line. His support and encouragement for this project was beyond measure. I love you very much and am so happy I married the RIGHT guy. (Luh!) I also can't thank my three beautiful children, Buddy, Grace, and Ted enough for their love and support. They put up with a lot of poorly-thought-out meals, unmade beds and late nights. (It's here where I should probably acknowledge "The Art of Entertaining" and Schwann's frozen food delivery service!) Kids, I am sorry about all the times I shushed you and kicked you out of my office because I was "working on the book!" I am so proud and happy to be your mom.

Love and thanks goes to my father, Jack Collins. Your example of what a good husband and father looks like surely stopped me from marrying the wrong guy. I am finally realizing the full measure of your sacrifice to raise two daughters and put them through private school and college. I love you! I am certain that my mother, on her heavenly perch somewhere, is aware of this book as well. She hasn't sent me my winning lottery numbers yet, but she did send me the title in a dream. Thanks, mom! We miss you.

Of course, I must recognize my wonderful co-author, Jennifer. I would not have been able to finish this book without you. I am so grateful for your support, professional wisdom and most importantly your friendship. You have so many wonderful qualities that balance out my own, shall we say, "quirkier" ones. What a team. It was so awesome to have my own therapist on standby 24 hours a day. Aren't you glad we went to Starbucks that day! (Thanks Mary Michalski!)

Thanks too, to all of my friends who had to listen to me talk about this project for so many years, particularly the I.C. I don't want to name names for fear of leaving anyone out. I do apologize for repeatedly sucking all of you into my "wedding vortex." I also appreciate those who forwarded my emails, surveys and questionnaires. Thanks for your part in finding such great stories. Many thanks go to my dear St. Joe friends who took the time to read and critique the book.

I want to give special credit to the fabulous faculty of St. Joseph's Academy in St. Louis. That is the place where I learned how to write. Any positive characteristics that I may have — that I did not receive from my family — came from my four years at St. Joe. I particularly want to thank Santa Cuddihee, Mary Alice Hennessy and Leah Preston for recognizing my abilities even though I was not at the top of my class. I am an example of what St. Joe can do for an intelligent, yet highly uninspired student. Thank you from the bottom of my A.D.D. heart.

I gratefully acknowledge my four years at Loyola University in New Orleans. While I loved Loyola, I suspect it was my time spent in the taverns and bars of Uptown New Orleans that really taught me how to tell a story and conduct an interview!

I would also like to recognize my amazing editors and copyeditors. Leslie Gibson McCarthy—if it wasn't for your wise advice, this book would have been nothing more than a "wordy sermon." Your insights put this project on the right track. You are an outstanding writer and now it's your turn to write a book. Many thanks also go to Rebekah Matt, "defender of the content." You zeroed in on so many key issues and offered razor-sharp advice. I also appreciate Dave Brumfield's eagle eye. As I always say about you, still waters run deep!

I also offer thanks to my professional helpers who did their part to bring this book to market: Christine Frank, Shelley Dieterichs, Linda Rivard and Nate Paul. If you need a book packager, a graphic designer, photographer or a web designer — these are the people to call. I must also thank Jane "Mary

Poppins" Tayon for her help and cheerleading. I am also very grateful to Bobby Linkemer and the St. Louis Publisher's Association.

I also promised to recognize my carpool: Grace, Teddy, Jack, Joel, Katelyn and Danny. Thank you for not saying anything to me about wearing the same sweat suit everyday or commenting about my hair standing straight up after long hours of writing. I really appreciate it.

Thanks go to my neighbors, the Timpes, for letting me sit by their pool and write. I also appreciate the staff of the Crestwood Starbucks for keeping "time on task" with countless venti whole milk lattes. And finally, I must acknowledge my two office assistants, Monsieur Le Choi and Mr. Dingo. You two kept me company for hours on end. (Side note: did you know that cats snore and dogs chase Frisbees in their dreams?)

This has been a really wonderful, fulfilling project and I am so thrilled to complete it. I hope you enjoy reading it. Most importantly, I hope it stops a whole lot of women from marrying the wrong guy!

Anne Milford
March 2009

Jennifer's Acknowledgements

First and foremost I want to thank the most important person in my life, my husband, Dan. Your love, your patience and your support have pushed me through this process in ways I cannot describe. We go together like "peas and carrots" and I can honestly say that I have never questioned whether or not you are the right guy. I can't wait to see what new adventures lie ahead for us. Most importantly I thank you for the gift of our children, Julia and Josh. What a surprise we had that day in the ultrasound room nine years ago! I have always known what a wonderful father you would be and I am so grateful that the three of us have you in our life.

Julia and Josh, my number one fans! Thank you for not complaining too much when I had to work on this project. I am honored to be your mom and to spend time with you enjoying the things you love most like reading, swimming, bike riding, hiking and geo caching. I know you don't always have clean socks to wear but you have been there cheering me on the whole way. Julia, I love your personal motto, "Believe what you believe. Don't believe what you don't believe." I know I believe in the two of you!

Now on to you, Anne. It has been an awesome and wild ride with you since our chance meeting at the Crestwood Starbuck's that cold December day. Our connection was instantaneous, and I am quite certain that we knew each other in a past life. I do not believe in coincidences, and it seems both of our paths have led us to this amazing accomplishment. You helped me uncover a creative part of myself that had been dormant for quite some time. I had forgotten about that 9 year old girl who wrote her first story in the third grade. She is so thankful to be rediscovered! Writing this book was a huge surprise in my life but an even better surprise is the friendship and partnership that was the ultimate end result. This is just the beginning for Cold Feet Press!

To my parents, Colleen Connelly and Bryan Nelson. I know the last 13+ years have not always been easy. I hope that you can find a way to see through my eyes as you read my words. You may not have been "right" for each other but hopefully you have now found the happiness you were looking for. I am sure I speak for my brother, Sean, when I say we are glad that we are a result of your marriage.

I need to send a thank you out to Dr. Richard Schwartz, founder of The Center for Self Leadership and the Internal Family Systems model. I have only met you a handful of times but your work has had such an impact on both my professional and personal life. I am thrilled to share some of that work with the world through this book. Thanks also to my Level 1 IFS group, especially my training staff, Paul Ginter, Elizabeth Taeubert, Mary DuParri, Mark Robinson, Marni Pearlman and Uri Talmor. Ironically the birth of this book coincided with my training and I am so grateful that it did, otherwise my critical parts would have totally halted my progress. I still have to remind myself that "All parts are welcome!"

There are several other "characters" in my story that I need to mention who have had an incredible impact on my life. They say teachers are our unsung heroes. So to every teacher who has ever touched my life, Thank you! However, the teacher who stands out most for me is my 10th grade English teacher, Ms. Gail Egleston. Your no nonsense attitude was exactly what I needed then and it helped me develop the writing skills that I continue to use today. You may not remember but you gave me a copy of *The Prophet* for graduation. Twenty years later I continue to treasure this gift. We even snuck in a quote in Chapter 8. I hope you are enjoying retirement and can find some joy in knowing what an important part you played in my journey.

Two other very important teachers I would like to acknowledge are Dr. Ann Dell Duncan and Dr. Wells Hively. You saw potential in me even before I did so many moons ago. Your clinical expertise and insight helped mold me as a person and helped me become the therapist I am today.

To all of my friends and colleagues, there are too many of you to mention by name, but you know who you are. You support has been astonishing. You responded to my countless emails and questionnaires. You patiently listened to my ideas and offered suggestions of your own. Many of you even shared your own personal relationship story for these very pages. I am truly blessed to have so many wonderful, wise and authentic people in my life.

And finally, thank you to all of the women whom I have never met or spoken to but who shared their story in this book. Thank you for your courage to answer an email from a complete stranger in an effort to help so many other women who are facing the exact same challenges in their relationships. Your stories are the most powerful piece of information a reader will take away from this book. We really do believe that if you understand how to marry the wrong guy, you will know how to marry the right one.

Jennifer Gauvain

March 2009

ANNE

Anne Milford canceled her wedding exactly five months before the big day. In the aftermath of her breakup, she realized how many people want to cancel their wedding —but don't. They plod along in unhealthy relationships and end up getting married — even though they know it's a big mistake. As everyone congratulated her on her bravery, she wondered why there wasn't a book about doomed-from-the-start relationships and marriages. Now, with over 20 years experience as a freelance writer and editor, and 15 years as a happily married woman — she has written that book. Milford has unveiled the real-life stories of women with either mistaken first marriages or canceled weddings. She also has interviewed dozens of women who describe themselves as happily wed. She believes that women can learn how to date or marry the right guy by understanding why women often marry the wrong one.

Milford earned her B.A. in Communications from Loyola University in New Orleans. She lives in St. Louis, Missouri with her husband, three children and dog, Dingo.

JENNIFER

Jennifer Gauvain is a licensed clinical social worker whose primary focus is working with couples and families. With over 13 years experience in private practice, she helps us interpret the stories gathered and addresses the issues revealed by those who forged ahead with a mistaken marriage. She also shares the wisdom she and her husband have gained on the marriage prep team at St. Francis Xavier College Church, in St. Louis, Mo. As the adult child of divorced parents, Jennifer has both personal and clinical insight into the destruction divorce sheds upon couples and families. Her clinical skills and expertise can help women who are struggling with their relationship or pending marriage to effectively discern what they are really searching for in their life.

Jennifer earned her M.S.W. from the George Warren Brown School of Social Work at Washington University in St. Louis, Mo. She continued her postgraduate training at The Menninger Relationship and Family Therapy Training Institute. She recently completed Internal Family Systems training through the Center for Self Leadership in Oak Park, Ill. Jennifer lives in St. Louis, with her husband, 8-year-old twins and dogs, Laney and Ginger.

Resources

Recommendations for Further Reading:

While conducting research for this book, we spent countless hours at the library, in book stores and on the Internet trying to increase our awareness of complicated relationship issues. If you enjoy reading as much as we do, we highly recommend the following books:

Behrendt, Greg & Tucillo, Liz (2004). *He's Just Not that Into You.*

Bloch, Douglas (1991). *Listening to Your Inner Voice: Discover the Truth Within You and Let It Guide Your Way.*

Branden, Nathaniel (1983). *Honoring the Self: Self-Esteem and Personal Transformation.*

Chodron, Pema (2001). *The Places That Scare You: A Guide to Fearlessness in Difficult Times.*

Cooper, Robert K. (2001). *The Other 90%.*

Devries, Susan & Mark, Wolgemuth, Bobbie & Robert (2003). *The Most Important Year In a Woman's Life, The Most Important Year In a Man's Life.*

Gigerezer, Gerd (2007). *Gut Feelings: The Intelligence of the Unconscious.*

Gilbert, Elizabeth (2006). *Eat, Pray, Love.*

Gottman, John & Silver, Nan (1999). *The Seven Principles For Making Marriage Work.*

Kerner, Ian (2005). *Be Honest-You're Not That Into Him Either: Raise Your Standards and Reach For the Love You Deserve.*

Lerner, Harriet (2001). *The Dance of Connection.*

Mayerson, Charlotte (1996). *Goin' to the Chapel: Dreams of Love, Realities of Marriage.*

Paul, Pamela (2002). *The Starter Marriage and the Future of Matrimony.*

Safier, Rachel with Roberts, Wendy (2003). *There Goes the Bride: Making Up Your Mind, Calling it Off and Moving On.*

Schwartz, Richard (2001). *Introduction to the Internal Family Systems Model.*

Schwartz, Richard (2008). *You Are the One You've Been Waiting For, Bringing Courageous Love to Intimate Relationships.*

Stern, Robin (2007). *The Gaslight Effect: How to Spot and Survive the Hidden Manipulation Others Use to Control Your Life.*

Stepp, Laura Sessions (2007). *Unhooked: How Young Women Pursue Sex, Delay Love and Lose at Both.*

Tolle, Eckhart (2005). *A New Earth: Awakening to Your Life's Purpose.*

Wallerstein, Judith S., & Blakeslee, Sandra (1995). *The Good Marriage: How and Why Love Lasts.*

Other Resources you may find helpful:

www.attractingthelifeyouwant.com (Ruby Slippers, LLC): Ruby Slippers, LLC helps women create and implement their personal life visions by connecting them first with their intuition, their most valuable asset. In retreats, workshops and presentations women learn how to use their intuition as a guide to designing a life that reflects what they want – not what somebody else wants for them! (info@attractingthelifeyouwant.com or call 207-443-2847)

www.selfleadership.org: Visit this Web site to learn more about the Internal Family Systems (IFS) model. Dr. Richard Schwartz describes his model in simple terms as "a conceptual framework and practice for developing love for ourselves and each other." You can also search the database of therapists who practice IFS.

www.smartmarriages.com: The Coalition for Marriage, Family and Couples Education. This Web site is packed with helpful resources — and it's not just for married people. There are books, articles, quotes and information on several different relationship courses. According to their Web site, the recommended resources and courses are for *any* couple at *any* stage – dating, engaged, newlywed, and cohabiting. They also offer distance-learning options.

www.kathyesper.com: Whether you're attracting the ideal man and/or the ideal clients, it all starts with illuminating your "Unique Presence" in the world, both practically and energetically. Visit Kathy Esper's Web site for more information and resources.

www.coldfeetpress.com: Visit our blog for more information about relationship issues.

Suggested Resources for Finding a Therapist:

The following Web sites can help you locate a therapist in your area. Refer back to Chapter 9 for detailed information on finding a qualified therapist.

www.psychologytoday.com: (Click on Find a Therapist)

www.find-a-therapist.com: Noted as the largest on-line database of therapy providers.

www.coldfeetpress.com: Jennifer Gauvain, co-author, is a Licensed Clinical Social Worker in private practice in St. Louis, Missouri. She also consults via telephone and Skype. Contact her via the Web site for more information.

Fax orders 1-877-252-4579 Send this form
Telephone orders: 1-877-239-2155 x1(Have your credit card ready.)
E-mail orders info@coldfeetpress.com

VISIT OUR WEB Site at www.coldfeetpress.com

Post Orders:
Cold Feet Press
8734 Norcross Drive
St Louis, MO 63126
1-877-239-2155 x1

Please send _____ (quantity) of **How to Marry the Wrong Guy:
A Guide for Avoiding the Biggest Mistake of Your Life**

SHIP TO: PLEASE NOTE IF THIS IS BEING SHIPPED
ANONYMOUSLY!

Name_____

Address_____

City_____ State_____ Zip_____

Telephone _____

E-mail Address
Sales Tax: Please add 7.825% sales tax for products shipped to Missouri
Addresses

Ground shipping rates: call 1-877-239-2155 x1 for shipping rates

coldfeetpress.com